# Hip-Hop Theology

# Hip-Hop Theology

*Only the Lover Raps*

EDITED BY
Claude Atcho
Alex Sosler

CASCADE *Books* · Eugene, Oregon

HIP-HOP THEOLOGY
Only the Lover Raps

Copyright © 2026 Wipf and Stock Publishers. All rights reserved. Except for brief quotations in critical publications or reviews, no part of this book may be reproduced in any manner without prior written permission from the publisher. Write: Permissions, Wipf and Stock Publishers, 199 W. 8th Ave., Suite 3, Eugene, OR 97401.

Cascade Books
An Imprint of Wipf and Stock Publishers
199 W. 8th Ave., Suite 3
Eugene, OR 97401

www.wipfandstock.com

PAPERBACK ISBN: 978-1-6667-8550-0
HARDCOVER ISBN: 978-1-6667-8551-7
EBOOK ISBN: 978-1-6667-8552-4

*Cataloguing-in-Publication data:*

Names: Atcho, Claude, editor. | Sosler, Alex, editor.

Title: Hip-hop theology : only the lover raps /Claude Atcho and Alex Sosler, editors.

Description: Eugene, OR: Cascade Books, 2026 | Includes bibliographical references.

Identifiers: ISBN 978-1-6667-8550-0 (paperback) | ISBN 978-1-6667-8551-7 (hardcover) | ISBN 978-1-6667-8552-4 (ebook)

Subjects: LCSH: Rap (Music)—Religious aspects—Christianity. | Hip-hop—Religious aspects—Christianity.

Classification: ML3921.8 H66 2026 (paperback) | ML3921.8 (ebook)

VERSION NUMBER 01/28/26

Scripture quotations marked NASB® taken from the New American Standard Bible®, Copyright © 1960, 1971, 1977, 1995, 2020 by The Lockman Foundation. Used by permission. All rights reserved. www.Lockman.org

Scripture quotations marked MSG are taken from The Message, copyright © 1993, 2002, 2018 by Eugene H. Peterson. Used by permission of NavPress. All rights reserved.

Scripture quotations marked ESV are from the ESV® Bible (The Holy Bible, English Standard Version®), © 2001 by Crossway, a publishing ministry of Good News Publishers. ESV Text Edition: 2025. Used by permission. All rights reserved

Scripture quotations marked (NLT) are taken from the Holy Bible, New Living Translation, copyright ©1996, 2004, 2015 by Tyndale House Foundation. Used by permission of Tyndale House Publishers, Carol Stream, Illinois 60188. All rights reserved.

# Contents

*List of Contributors* | vii

Introduction | 1

## Part One: Call

1 Profanely Prophetic | 15
  —Dwight Radcliff

2 Lyrical Location: Hip-Hop Artists as Patriots? | 33
  —Alex Sosler

## Part Two: Response

3 Eschatological Flow: Theology, Temporality, and Rhythm in OutKast's "Rosa Parks" | 51
  —C. M. Howell

4 From good kid to Wounded Healer: Examining Kendrick Lamar's Approach to Trauma, Vocation, and Healing | 70
  —Claude Atcho

5 Back on Beat: A Theology of Socioeconomics and Solidarity in Akrobatik's "Remind My Soul" | 87
  —Krystal Berry

6 The Voice of Wisdom Cries Out: Poetic, Prophetic Proverbs | 106
—Alex Sosler

## Part Three: Testimony

7 Why? A Theological Reflection of Jadakiss's Most
Thought-Provoking Questions | 125
—Nicole Hudnell

8 The Theology of Suffering and Songs for This Age | 140
—Stephanie Laferriere Greer

# List of Contributors

Dwight Radcliff is assistant professor of mission, theology and culture and the academic dean for the Pannell Center for Black Church Studies at Fuller Theological Seminary. He has authored several chapters and essays in his fields, and he pastors the Message Center in Southern California.

C. M. Howell (PhD, University of St. Andrews) is a research assistant for the Widening Horizons in Continental Philosophy project. Prior to his academic pursuit, he worked as a professional musician, alongside a career in architecture. He is the author of the forthcoming monographs *Too Sick to Pray: A Theology of Outlaw Country* (Fortress, 2026) and *Beauty in the Absence of God: The Theological Aesthetics of Eberhard Jüngel* (Mohr Siebeck, 2026).

Krystal Berry is a native of Southampton County, Virginia, by way of Houston, Texas, an itinerant minister, and the current associate director of Black Church Studies at Duke University Divinity School. She is pursuing doctoral studies in Old Testament theological interpretation with a focus on literary archeology and historical reconstructionism.

Claude Atcho is rector at Church of the Resurrection in Charlottesville, Virginia, as well as author of *Reading Black Books* and *Rhythms of Faith*.

## List of Contributors

Nicole Hudnell (DMin, Liberty University) is the self-proclaimed "Daughter of Hip-Hop." She is the founder of the Hip Hop Ed youth program and nonprofit organization The HERC based in her hometown of the Bronx, New York. She received her doctorate in Next Generation Ministry focusing on hip-hop theology.

Stephanie Greer lives in Baltimore, Maryland, with her family and serves as a gospel worker for ONE HOPE (www.onehope.gives). She's passionate about people, coffee, and dope flowers that God has created.

Alex Sosler is associate professor of Bible and ministry at Montreat College and assisting priest at Redeemer Anglican Church in Asheville, North Carolina.

# Introduction

TWO ANGLICAN PRIESTS WALK into an art workshop. It could be the start of a joke, but it's the genesis of *Hip-Hop Theology*. (Could there be anything less hip-hop than Anglicanism?) But here we are. By happenstance, we met at the Glen Workshop hosted by *Image Journal*. A generative conversation started there that became the idea for this book. We come to hip-hop from different perspectives.

## FROM CLAUDE

It's common for Christians to pray for a child to grow up never knowing a day apart from God's love. While that prayer came true for me, I also never knew a day apart from hip-hop as a soundtrack to my life. Summer visits to my aunt and uncle in Pasadena, California, ensured a healthy dose of 90s' Death Row Records. A summer stay in Newark, New Jersey, and a few forays into NYC in 1996 meant an introduction to "Hot 97" and an infatuation with *It Was Written* and the shiny suit era of Bad Boy Records. From there, I snagged Tupac's *Greatest Hits*, playing "Trapped" on repeat daily before getting absorbed in the debut records of Lil Wayne before turning to underground rap in late high school with the self-righteousness of hip-hop Pharisee. At every turn in my journey, hip-hop has been essential, expanding my world, challenging

Introduction

my perspective, and connecting me in surprising ways with others who the music and its expansive culture have shaped.

## FROM ALEX

I had a different introduction to hip-hop. I stumbled upon the hip-hop world in a similar way to another outsider named Rick Rubin. A white, scraggly punk rocker, Rubin discovered the early artists of hip-hop and helped produce the iconic sound of the Beastie Boys, Run DMC, and others. The first two CDs I remember buying in one of those magazine-ordering catalogs were Green Day's *Nimrod* and Tupac's *Greatest Hits*. I was drawn to the subversive. I loved the poetry of Tupac's language and voice and the grunge sound of punk rock. For me, those on the margins drew me in. They were saying something, rebelling against the mainline in a way that I found compelling. Particularly with Tupac, he was lamenting but latent with hope. Something about his rawness was provocative and offensive but revealed something I couldn't see any other way. From Tupac, I found the lyrical complexity of the Roots. From the Roots, my love for Trap music and beats developed as I moved from Lil' Flip to Lil Wayne. As an outsider, I view my work in this volume similarly to Rubin's. I don't reside in the same culture, but I want to exalt the black and brown voices who have something for us to hear. I want to hear the heartbeat of this culture and make it sing. I'm honored that these contributors have trusted me with their voices.

Regardless of how either of us arrived at hip-hop, we both had to determine how hip-hop fits within our Christianity. I remember feeling a rub between the two: can hip-hop beats be sanctified? Can perverse lyrics serve the kingdom? The central question that animates the following project is this: "What has Jerusalem to do with the Bronx, or Compton, or the South Side of Chicago, or the west side of Houston?" Senior scholars, emerging scholars, and practitioners have joined voices to help answer these questions.

## THE RIGHT TIME

Rap recently celebrated its fiftieth anniversary from its Sedgwick Avenue beginning in 1973. It's been over fifty years of beats, breaks, and raps. We stand on the shoulders of this rich heritage, and this rich heritage of

Introduction

theological commentary on hip-hop—from Ralph Basui Watkins[1] and Daniel White Hodge[2] to Andre Johnson.[3] We want to expand their work rather than replace it.

Fifty years has also brought a change to the cultural reception of hip-hop. Even in the past ten years, hip-hop has increasingly crossed boundaries. A recent adaptation of the comic book series Spiderman had a hip-hop soundtrack and featured a black lead (*Into the Spiderverse*, 2018). Perhaps the most well-known Broadway musical (of all things!) in recent history had a heavy dose of hip-hop (*Hamilton*, 2015). Hip-hop has spread to such disparate cultures like comic books and musicals. A long way from Sedgwick Ave. in 1973!

Further, the "higher" arts have begun recognizing hip-hop as poetry. In 2018, Kendrick Lamar won the coveted and renowned Pulitzer Prize for his record *DAMN*. He was the first rap artist to win the award. Culture is starting to recognize the depth that hip-hop has. Sure, there are artists that center on swag and vibe. (And there's a place for that!) But in this volume, we focus on those who are true poets and storytellers.

So, for all these recent reasons, we felt it was time to continue discussing theology's relation and interplay in and with hip-hop.

## TOWARD A REDEMPTIVE MODEL OF ART

What does it mean to make "Christian" or "theological" art? Does it need John 3:16 in the lyrics? Does it need to mention God? Does it need "spiritual" themes? Does it need lyrics at all?

We want to broaden our understanding of "Christian" art. We prefer the term "redemptive" art. What kind of art is redemptive, that leads us higher, that helps us be more whole? For this, a Christian witness can be much more holistic, and even those who claim no faith at all can be redemptive artists. Like the poets of Greece in Areopagus (Acts 17), they can testify to the truth of God even if in part. What follows is a typology to understand a full, holistic Christian witness:

---

1. Watkins, *Hip-Hop Redemption*.
2. Hodge, *Soul of Hip Hop*.
3. Johnson, *Urban God Talk*.

# Introduction

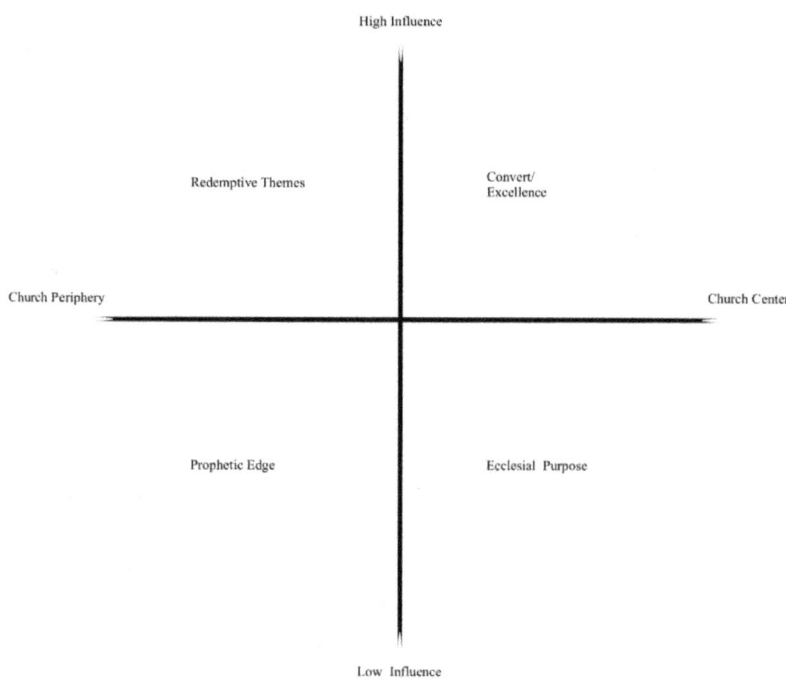

Oftentimes, those interested in theology and the arts will want to segment Christian art into one corner. I want to show that each aspect of redemptive art is valuable in itself and that we need not narrow our conception of what "Christian" is; hence, my use of the broader "redemptive" term rather than "Christian."

The right side of the graph is where most Christian conversations stay. Christians can often find these artists more comfortable, either artists who have converted to Christianity or those who make art for the church. There's nothing wrong with this horizontal axis, but it tends to focus on the artists' content or personal life in a highly defined way. Ambiguity is often a source of criticism. That's why the horizontal access is labeled "church center" and "church periphery." Those on the right side of the graph have more "play" or understanding within the church than the left half. Typically, the left side of the graph has a bit more complexity to their art form as well, which accounts for them not being as "popular" or "accessible."

The vertical axis is based on popularity. Those on the top half have more listeners and influence than those on the bottom half. I think this can apply to all forms of art (visual, poetic, and other music genres) but for the

Introduction

sake of this project, I'll apply an individual hip-hop artist to each type. It's important to note, too, that this is a mere conceptual scheme. Artists often do not neatly fall into a category, so these lines are blurry more than they are clear. And then some artists defy categorization. Where would an artist like U2 fit? (Probably between Convert/Excellence and Redemptive Theme.) Or Tupac Shakur? (Maybe between Convert/Excellence and Prophetic Edge.) Regardless, I think this typology can be a starting point from which we see various generative redemptive witnesses in the life of the culture.

## Convert/Excellence

I label the top right corner as the "Convert/Excellence" witness of Christianity because I think two kinds of people can exist in this highly influential and ecclesial quadrant. On the one hand, an artist can make it to the top of their craft and then convert to Christianity. In a different genre, an example could be someone like Bob Dylan. Or, an artist can rise to the top of their craft while being explicitly Christian. Someone like Beethoven for classical music (though the culture was different) or Makoto Fujimura in the visual arts come to mind. They are people who do their craft excellently and are respected by those who do not believe in Jesus because they are so good at what they do. These both represent an unapologetic witness to Christianity at the center of culture. Perhaps, Kanye West can be seen as someone who has become a cultural witness to Christianity at the center of culture. Regardless of how we evaluate Kanye's conversion, he has a stage with (sometimes) explicitly Christian lyrics that few have. It's one way to make redemptive art: from the cultural center.

James Davison Hunter in *To Change the World* argues that changing the world happens from the top down rather than the popular model of the bottom up.[4] Those who are culture changers exist and influence the top levels of cultural formation. In this sense, it's good to have a witness at the center of culture: LA, Hollywood, New York. Culture spreads from these important cultural hubs.

There are inherent dangers in this type of cultural impact, of course. Often, the church uses these converts as a type of pawn in the cultural influence game, as if having someone at the top of their craft gives more credibility to the gospel than others. We can assume too much from recent converts in being more spiritually and morally mature than they can be.

4. Hunter, *To Change the World*.

These over-realized hopes can be dashed if they make mistakes or renounce the faith eventually, not to mention the general damage of celebrity culture.[5] Sometimes, culture influences them more than they influence culture. Nevertheless, those artists in the top right quadrant do add something to the Christian witness to culture in the reach they have.

## Redemptive Themes

An artist in the top left corner may not have the explicit lyrics or album that those on the right side may create. However, they may have songs that deal with salvation or faith or a redemptive theme. In these ways, they provide expressions of humanistic concerns that all image-bearers of God share.

I lived in Austin when Chance the Rapper headlined the Austin City Limits concert festival. In the same week, I was in a church context advocating for Chance's redemptive, though at times contradicting, witness. He was on *Late Night with Stephen Colbert* and performed an unreleased song called "First World Problems." The set moved from dark to light as he moved from lament to joy. There was nothing explicitly Christian, yet the redemptive themes were powerful and evident. The church wasn't buying it, though.

The next week, I was sitting at lunch on the University of Texas campus. I overheard a conversation about Chance the Rapper. The bartender was looking forward to Chance coming into town. She loved his *Acid Rap*. But, she said, "he's gotten too religious."

So, for my Christian friend, Chance the Rapper isn't Christian enough. To the person who is not a Christian, he's too Christian. So, which it is? It's no easy question, and why do these in the redemptive space add something necessarily complex to a robust Christian witness?

## Prophetic Edge

With artists in the Redemptive Theme and Prophetic Edge corners, they function a bit like "border stalkers" to coin a phrase from Makoto Fujimura.[6] They aren't quite comfortable in the mainstream of culture or the mainstream of the church. They exist at the periphery, away from the centers.

---

5. See Beaty, *Celebrities for Jesus*.
6. Fujimura, *Culture Care*, 106.

# Introduction

They can see a bit more clearly when not trying to make their art form to any particular cultural center. The more complex and robust art is made in these areas.

Kendrick Lamar is a fitting figure in the Prophetic Edge (though his performance in the 2025 Super Bowl is challenging my "not as popular" quadrant). Christians typically don't accept him, and he challenges popular notions in culture. Whereas redemptive thematic artists can tend to have more positive themes, those with a prophetic edge can tend to be a bit harsher. He's popular but also subversive. Kendrick's rhymes are not easy if by easy we mean simple to interpret. Yet he adds depth to the Christian witness, a truth-telling that sometimes the church can neglect or at least polish before saying. James Cone noted, "Black artists are prophetic voices whose calling requires them to speak truth to power. Their expressions are not controlled by the sanitation of the church. More than anyone, artists demonstrate our understanding of the need to represent the beauty and the terror of our people's experience."[7] Kendrick is at the edge telling it like reality is, a prophetic voice upsetting our expectations. This dynamic makes him an endearing witness, and a complicated one.

## Ecclesial Purpose

Lastly, the Ecclesial Purpose is art used within and for the church. Typically, this art is the most simple and easiest to bypass or critique. The 1980s Christian rock artist Larry Norman calls this art as propaganda. It reduces complexity to tell us what to believe. There's nothing wrong with this type of art, but it tends to be the least interesting.

A rapper like Trip Lee would fit comfortably within the Ecclesial Purpose quadrant. The church needs art geared toward the church. She needs art tethered and grounded in theological truth. Singing Kendrick Lamar in a Sunday service would rightfully feel odd. So, the Ecclesial Purpose fills a role within a full Christian witness, but often, this is seen as "the way" to do Christian art, which I think is limiting.

For the sake of this project, we'll be focusing on the first three quadrants as we analyze and interpret hip-hop: the Convert/Excellence, the Redemptive Theme, and the Prophetic Edge. All three provide different redemptive lenses for thinking about artistic expression in hip-hop.

---

7. Cone, *Cross and the Lynching Tree*, 118–19.

Introduction

**KEEPING IT REAL**

Along with reading hip-hop redemptively, a theological understanding of hip-hop can come from listening to the human experience, specifically those coming from black and brown communities, and often from poverty. With a theological lens, we should want to hear from those "least of these" where the face of Christ is seen (Matt 25).

In James Cone's *The Spirituals and the Blues*, he argues that "black music is the music of the soul."[8] Black music comes from the depths—whether the depths be slavery in the spirituals, societal bondage in the blues, or the pain of the black experience today in hip-hop. In many ways, this work extends the work of Cone from the blues to hip-hop. In hip-hop, we get another lens and testimony to the black experience. It may be something that makes us uncomfortable, at times perverse. The blues were about dealing with the black experience now, as it is, rather than escaping to some terrestrial paradise. Likewise, we need to reckon with one's own lived experiences, as despairing as they can be, yet as ones without final despair. W. E. B. Du Bois described sorrow songs in *The Souls of Black Folk*: "They are the music of an unhappy people, of the children of disappointment; they tell of death and suffering and unvoiced longing toward a truer world, of misty wanderings and hidden ways."[9] As such, black music as soul music is often in the minor key.

But again, with Christian theology, we must not overlook these realities, even if we would rather ignore them. Many of these contributors bear the pain that hip-hop bears. That's what good art does. An artist displays their soul, not as a pure act of self-expression like a diary entry, but so that others can listen in and say, "You, too? You've experienced that, too? I thought I was the only one, and you expressed the depths of my soul that were too hard for me to articulate." Hip-hop can do that. Hip-hop artists keep it real.

Sometimes, that pain feels on the verge of voyeurism. I (Alex) remember listening to Immortal Technique's "Dance with the Devil" for the first time, where he documents a gang initiation. I'll save the details, but it is intimate and disturbing. I felt like I shouldn't be listening in, like it was an experience too close to tell about. Sometimes, true art does that—it crosses a boundary of which we would rather stay on the opposite side.

8. Cone, *Spirituals and the Blues*, 104.
9. Du Bois, "Sorrow Songs."

## Introduction

Other times, we need that truth-telling to shake us from complacency. Of all unlikely places, Flannery O'Connor's literary theory can help us understand how the grotesque can reveal. O'Connor displayed the grotesque to shock her contemporaries awake. She displayed true reality unadulterated—in all its complexity and ambiguity. We need to sit in another's experience to see. Kendrick Lamar similarly uses the grotesque. In his most recent album, he displays the intense relational conflict in "We Cry Together." His content is not neat and clean. His language is crass. But he reveals something real and true. And like O'Connor's contemporaries, many in the church may think, "Must redemption include the ugly? Does the cross have to be crass? Shouldn't there be a happy ending?" And O'Connor says she writes with the grotesque because she's a Christian.[10] The cross is our paradigm of beauty. The most heinous event in human history becomes our new model of beauty. Beauty is grotesque, misshapen, and harsh. Hip-hop can display that complicated beauty, and Christians are invited to listen to the experience of the real. "It is only in his music," wrote James Baldwin, "which Americans are able to admire because a protective sentimentality limits their understanding of it, that the Negro in America has been able to tell his story."[11]

In *Hip-Hop Theology*, we seek to evaluate artists on their own accord. This way of looking at theology is seeing the theology that emerges within the hip-hop community rather than imposing a theology on hip-hop culture. Thus, hip-hop and theology are a dialogical work of cultural theology: theology affects how we understand the culture, and culture can help us articulate and see some theological concepts. They were in harmonious

---

10. See O'Connor, "On Her Own Work"; and "The Church and the Fiction Writer," in *Mystery and Manners*.

Another example is from a letter to a young reader on July 20, 1955. She writes, "I write the way I do because (not though) I am a Catholic. This is a fact and nothing covers it like the bald statement. However, I am a Catholic peculiarly possessed of the modern consciousness, that thing Jung describes as unhistorical, solitary, and guilty. To possess this within the Church is to bear a burden, the necessary burden for the conscious Catholic. It's to feel the contemporary situation at the ultimate level. I think that the Church is the only thing that is going to make the terrible world we are coming to endurable; the only thing that makes the Church endurable is that it is somehow the body of Christ and that on this we are fed. It seems to be a fact that you have to suffer as much from the Church as for it but if you believe in the divinity of Christ, you have to cherish the world at the same time that you struggle to endure it. This may explain the lack of bitterness in the stories" (O'Connor, *Habit of Being*, 90).

11. Baldwin, *Notes of a Native Son*, 25.

## Introduction

conflict with one another, and what emerges is a deeper and more generous theological imagination.

The book is divided into three parts: Call, Response, and Testimony. In the Call, Dwight Radcliff leads by exploring the profane in hip-hop and how Christians are invited to participate in the profane. Alex Sosler then follows with a discussion of hip-hop artists' urban localism and their love of place. Because they love their place, they have a right to critique it.

In part 2, we move from general discussion to a more close reads approach where contributors analyze specific artists or themes. In chapter 3, C. M. Howell gives a musical read of OutKast's "Rosa Parks" with an eye toward ultimate restoration. Next, Claude Atcho analyzes Kendrick Lamar's witness throughout his discography. Krystal Berry takes us on a journey to Boston to investigate the life and lyrics of Akrobatik's social commentary in chapter 5. In the final chapter of part 2, Alex Sosler examines the proverbial wisdom of rappers Chance the Rapper, Killer Mike, and Tobe Nwigwe.

In the final part, we have two "Testimonies," which are oriented toward the praxis or use of hip-hop in life and ministry. First, in chapter 7, Nicole Hudnell explores the questions that Jadakiss brings to the front and how that helps her unpack her own questions. The final chapter, written by Stephanie Laferriere Greer, testifies to the way hip-hop has helped her understand her own suffering and pain.

### ONLY THE LOVER RAPS

A final note on the subtitle. It's a riff from philosopher Joseph Pieper, who titled one of his books *Only the Lover Sings*. He draws from Gen 2 when God asks Adam to name things. He suggests that only lovers name things. Hip-hop names the beautiful and the broken, and we invite you to pay attention to what is named.

Our naming in this volume is by no means an attempt to be exhaustive. Each new year brings a plethora of new artists and new songs that provoke reflection. Our humble hope in this book is to give some fresh overview of the genre and to provide some proverbial tools to read the music with generosity and generativity.

We invite you to read, consider, and, if nothing else, to listen.

# Introduction

## BIBLIOGRAPHY

Baldwin, James. *Notes of a Native Son*. Boston: Beacon, 2012.

Beaty, Katelyn. *Celebrities for Jesus: How Personas, Platforms, and Profits Are Hurting the Church*. Grand Rapids: Brazos, 2022.

Cone, James. *The Cross and the Lynching Tree*. Maryknoll, NY: Orbis, 2013.

———. *The Spirituals and the Blues*. Maryknoll, NY: Orbis, 1991.

Du Bois, W. E. B. "Sorrow Songs." https://teachingamericanhistory.org/document/the-sorrow-songs/.

Fujimura, Makoto. *Culture Care: Reconnecting with Beauty for Our Common Life*. Downers Grove, IL: InterVarsity, 2017.

Hodge, Daniel White. *The Soul of Hip Hop: Rims, Timbs and a Cultural Theology*. Downers Grove, IL: InterVarsity, 2010.

Hunter, James Davison. *To Change the World: The Irony, Tragedy, and Possibility of Christianity in the Late Modern World*. New York: Oxford University Press, 2010.

Johnson, Andre. *Urban God Talk: Constructing a Hip Hop Spirituality*. Lanham, MD: Lexington, 2013.

O'Connor, Flannery. *The Habit of Being: Letters of Flannery O'Connor*. Edited by Sally Fitzgerald. New York: Farrar, Straus and Giroux, 1979.

———. *Mystery and Manners: Occasional Prose*. Edited by Sally Fitzgerald and Robert Fitzgerald. New York: Farrar, Straus and Giroux, 1969.

Watkins, Ralph Basui. *Hip-Hop Redemption: Finding God in the Rhythm and Rhyme*. Grand Rapids: Baker Academic, 2011.

# Part One

## Call

# 1

# Profanely Prophetic

### Dwight Radcliff

> Broken glass everywhere people pissing in the
> street you know they just don't care.
>
> —Grandmaster Flash and the Furious Five, "The Message"

> Prepare and eat this food as you would barley cakes. While all the people are watching, bake it over a fire using dried human dung as fuel and then eat the bread.
>
> —Ezekiel 4:12 (NLT)

The general narrative regarding Christian engagement of hip-hop is that hip-hop is unworthy of serious Christian or theological engagement. This posture is usually undergirded by a reductionist view of hip-hop as a genre of music that is simply vulgar and profane. When hip-hop is diminished to a category within the music production industry—or even to music in general—we lose the significance of hip-hop globally, and we lose sight of the people that hip-hop, in very real ways, represents and speaks

## Part One: Call

for. Hip-hop is music, true, but it is more than music. It is a style, a way of being in the world, a mentality, a billion-dollar global industry, a language, a genre of music, a way to express art, a style of dance, an oral history, and even a prophetic voice. At its core, hip-hop is a culture that seeks to express a lifestyle, a worldview, an attitude, and a search for God that rejects the oppression of the dominant culture and seeks to prioritize Black and Diasporic voices from the margins along with their histories, experiences, realities, and perceptions. The primary language of this culture is indeed musical, poetic, and artistic in nature. It borrows heavily from traditions rooted in the African Diaspora. By asserting hip-hop as a culture, I mean there is a particular worldview shaped and influenced by hip-hop. I also mean there are shared experiences, language, expressions, images, and histories that are part of the culture.

When hip-hop is understood in this greater context, it becomes difficult to adhere to a position of avoidance on the part of the serious Christian. I contend that if we take seriously the omnipresence of God and the *imago Dei* in all humans, then there is but one response to hip-hop—we must listen, and we must engage. To be clear, this call is not a mandate for every Christian to become an expert in hip-hop culture, rather, it is an explicit corrective to the narrative that hip-hop must be avoided at all costs for the sake of perceived purity or constructed holiness within the Christian journey. Hip-hop can be graphic, vulgar, and profane, but so is life, and so are the pages of our sacred Scriptures. It is intriguing—and probably somewhat hypocritical—how we embrace problematic, violent, and graphic portions of the Bible with no hesitation or caution. Yet we say that hip-hop cannot be touched for the same reasons. I say, again, hip-hop can be profane. However, listen we must. Ignoring difficult, painful, and complicated portions of life is escapism, not a Spirit-filled life of declaring good news. This chapter seeks to lay out a foundation for how we can and why should listen to hip-hop. The first section will build a foundation of suspended judgment that can enable us to listen deeply to content without immediate condemnation. This section will also attempt to argue a theological and missiological rationale for engagement. The second section will define and describe "the prophetic" in broader biblical terms to help reset our imaginations and understandings. By placing Marvin McMickle, Abraham Heschel, and Walter Brueggemann in conversation, I hope to demonstrate the profane and unpopular position and ministry of biblical prophets. Interwoven throughout this chapter and in its headings are some of the graphic texts and mandates from God. The chapter will close out with examples of theological assumptions that are being declared in, or can be interpreted from, hip-hop.

> Here on Earth, tell me what's a Black life worth. A bottle of juice is no excuse, the truth hurts. And even when you take the shit, move counties, get a lawyer, you can shake the shit. Ask Rodney, Latasha, and many more. It's been goin' on for years, there's plenty more. When they ask me, "When will the violence cease?" When your troops stop shootin n***** down in the street.
> —2Pac, "I Wonder if Heaven Got a Ghetto"

> And you, Babylonians—ravagers! A reward to whoever gets back at you for all you've done to us; Yes, a reward to the one who grabs your babies and smashes their heads on the rocks!
> —Ps 137:8–9 (MSG)

Michael Eric Dyson says that many people lack "a capacity for deferred justification. . . . They seek to ensure the legitimacy of their moral critique by rendering quick and easy judgments about [hip-hop]."[1] Dyson calls for "ethical patience" when engaging hip-hop so one can hear and seek to understand before issuing a moral decree.[2] Ralph Watkins elaborates on Dyson's ethical patience by asking readers/listeners to seek understanding and empathy with hip-hop—both the art and the lived experiences it represents.[3] Christians engaging hip-hop must stow away their luggage of orthodoxy and righteous indignation in order to hear the cries of humans made in the image of God.

Ethical patience does not require one to change theological positioning, necessarily. It does, however, require restraint; the ability to hear a complete thought or entire argument through without interrupting. Ethical patience assumes, correctly, that God is present with all humanity and that hip-hop is no different. Further, it asserts that hip-hop has something of value to say. As mentioned in this chapter's introduction, we have to name and expose our own hypocrisy when it comes to hip-hop. The revelation of God given to us in Scripture is sacred, but it also contains rape, murder, genocide, child abuse, misogyny, patriarchy, slavery, ethnocentrism, and other atrocities. More recent tragedies like the Holocaust, genocides in

---

1. Dyson, *Holler If You Hear Me*, 118.
2. Dyson, *Holler If You Hear Me*, 118.
3. Watkins, *Hip-Hop Redemption*, xi.

Rwanda and Armenia, or rises in sex trafficking are all things that Christians feel compelled to lean into and hear their horrific narratives; and rightly so. Hip-hop, however, gets summarily dismissed as unworthy of Christian attention, and the reasons given—as previously stated—are often the very reasons other narratives are centered. One can only imagine that, perhaps, the larger American tendency to silence and dismiss Black pain is at least part of the rationale.

It has been said that the church does not have a mission but that God's mission has a church. If the church is a tool or partner in God's mission, then the church must be engaged in the *missio Dei* to be considered an authentic church. It is widely agreed that Jesus' *magnum opus* is located in Luke 4:18-19: the proclamation of good news to the poor, liberty to the captives, sight to the blind, and freedom for the oppressed. If God's mission in the world can be, at least in some ways, summed up here in the words of Christ, then the gospel that the church declares and demonstrates must include good news to the poor, liberation, and healing. Even a cursory examination of Jesus' ministry method reveals this impetus.

Picture for a moment two popular instances of encounters with Jesus. In Matt 8, large crowds (of mostly, or large populations of, Jewish followers) are accompanying Jesus when he encounters a Roman centurion. Here is this man who represents the very oppression of Jesus' people. There is no doubt that some are waiting for Jesus to condemn this Roman representative of oppression, even if he has done some good deeds in the community. Jesus avoids the very real sociopolitical divides to attend to the pain of this human. Jesus stops and listens attentively. He suspends judgment and responds to the needs.

John 8 sets a scene of Jesus in the temple complex lecturing to a crowd. A woman caught in adultery is set in his midst—without the man, mind you—and the religious leaders challenge Jesus with the law's requirement to stone her. In this very public forum, Jesus could have returned to his lecture, but he chose to engage this complicated issue of sexual immorality, misogyny, and patriarchy. Jesus says that whoever is perfect can line up to throw the first rock as he stoops and writes in the ground. The men leave one by one, and Jesus tells the woman that he does not condemn her. The recorded Gospels show Jesus intentionally leaning in and listening time and time again. Whether being touched by and engaging a woman with a prolonged menstrual flow or going to a well in the afternoon to talk to a woman who was treated like a social pariah, Jesus repeatedly leans in, listens, and responds.

As Jesus models, following God's mission is not done by staying within the sanctified encampments of our cathedrals or within the margins of a predetermined orthodoxy. Rather, Jesus enters into the spaces of those considered off-limits with great regularity; much to the chagrin of the religious leaders of his time. It would seem that to follow in Christ's example would necessarily mean to engage those most in need of good news. Just as the Samaritan patches the wounds of the man left for dead, so should Christians be seeking to be a balm for those on the margins and in the ditches of life. One would be hard-pressed to defend a biblical hermeneutic of ignoring experiences of pain and systems of oppression. Not everyone is called to change policy, speak to governors, or change entire systems. But all Jesus' followers are called to lean in, to listen, and to respond with good news.

How do we listen, though, when the language and content are so explicit and offensive? The noted scholar Michael Eric Dyson gives us this for consideration: "What I'm concerned about is the necessity to hear from those young voices, sometimes bitter voices, sometimes voices that are dipped into the deep pools of profanity, sometimes vulgarity. But I'm not so much concerned about the curse words, as the cursed worlds they occupy, and what hurt they experience in order to produce some of the deeply reflective, deeply self-critical, and also deeply problematic lyrics that they put forth."[4] Dyson is asking about the hypocrisy of our offense. How are we offended by words and not by worlds?

> Alls my life I has to fight, N\*\*\*\*. Alls my life, I. Hard times like, Yah. Bad trips like, Yah. Nazareth, I'm f\*\*\*\* up. Homie, you f\*\*\*\* up. But if God got us, then we gon' be aright.
> —Kendrick Lamar, "Alright"

> Hear this word, you cows of Bashan who are on the mountain of Samaria, who oppress the poor, who crush the needy, who say to your husbands, "Bring now, that we may drink." The Lord God has sworn by His holiness, "Behold, the days are coming upon you when they will take you away with meat hooks, and the last of you with fish hooks."
> —Mic 4:1–2 (NASB)

---

4. Dyson, *Debating Race*, 232.

## Part One: Call

If we listen deeply, though, what are we listening to or for? I hold—and I'm not alone—that hip-hop is intrinsically prophetic. The culture is birthed amid a particular set of socioeconomic and political realities that birthed a culture that valued itself and its contributions in the face of layered systems that denied the same. Tricia Rose details that hip-hop, "Situated at the 'crossroads of lack and desire,' emerges from the deindustrialization meltdown where social alienation, prophetic imagination, and yearning intersect."[5] I do not intend to infer that every word spoken by every hip-hop artist is prophetic; no more than I would dare infer that every word spoken by someone who calls themselves a preacher is from God. I do hold, explicitly, that God does speak in and through hip-hop in ways that challenge broken systems, bring attention to voiceless populations, and highlight experiences that mar individuals' ability to live out the image of God in them. Hip-hop is profane—and prophetic.

## PROPHETIC HIP-HOP

What does it mean to say that hip-hop is prophetic? Let's define the term "prophetic." Time and space in this one chapter will not allow an extensive treatment so, for some, the following may feel concise and perhaps reductionist. Abraham Heschel, Walter Brueggemann, and Marvin McMickle are three scholars who have each written influential works on the prophetic but in very different ways. McMickle utilizes a Black theological hermeneutic that sees Jesus as the central prophetic figure and evaluates the prophetic nature of the Black preaching tradition.[6] Abraham Heschel urges that the Old Testament prophets themselves should be central.[7] Brueggemann, however, contends that we go back further to Moses.[8] Each of these perspectives and researchers represents particular lenses used to view the prophetic in Scripture and in the world. The goal here is to briefly put them in communication with each other. This conversation allows them to engage and critique one another; not for the sake of dominance, but in an honest dialogue from various perspectives and with their lenses confessed, to help us reach a more nuanced understanding.

---

5. Rose, *Black Noise*, 21.
6. McMickle, *Where Have All the Prophets Gone?*
7. Heschel, *Prophets*.
8. Brueggemann, *Prophetic Imagination*.

Heschel's work looks at the person and psychological experience of the prophet. The experiences and trauma of the biblical prophets shaped how they interacted with God and how they critiqued their religious and governmental powers via God's visions and messages. The very unorthodox methods of Hosea and Amos are due in part to God's selection/calling but also in part to the temperament and humanity of the individuals. Heschel understands God's agency within marginalized communities to speak on God's behalf: "The voice that God has lent to the silent agony, a voice to the plundered poor, to the profaned riches of the world."[9]

Brueggemann's approach, on the other hand, is to provide a definition of prophetic, and then to apply said definition to the act of preaching and the consciousness of the church. The initial lectures that would birth two books were delivered to ministers from the United Church of Christ and Disciples of Christ denominations and at North Park Seminary. Brueggemann sees the prophetic as God-given consciousness that is at odds with the consciousness of the larger society. He does so, however, without the advantage of a specifically African American heritage.[10] The work of Black thought leaders such as McMickle, or Cornel West and Theophus Smith, must be allowed to engage—and even critique—Brueggemann. This process is vital not because of Brueggemann's lack of "Blackness" but precisely because the other scholars have a cultural understanding of the prophetic that is rooted in the African American experience—the seedbed of hip-hop culture. McMickle explicitly deals with the prophetic nature of Black preaching. In this tradition, the African American preacher stands as a type of griot or shaman.[11] To put it more explicitly, the preacher comes forth from the tradition of the Hebrew prophet and not the Greek orator.[12] This understanding of the preacher as a conjurer of imaginations and divine trumpeter, rather than logical explicator, connects the Black preaching tradition to the biblical prophets for McMickle. This sounds similar—although not completely so—to Brueggemann's prophetic imagination. However, this may seem to deviate from Heschel's work in that the ministries and messages of the prophets are often viewed through a lens of liberation, and not one of Old Testament studies—which has its own embedded lens rooted in a majority European interpretive community.

9. Heschel, *Prophets*, 5.
10. Brueggemann, *Prophetic Imagination*; *Practice of Prophetic Imagination*.
11. Dyson, *Michael Eric Dyson Reader*; Smith, *Conjuring Culture*.
12. Moyd, *Sacred Art*, 56; Forsyth, *Positive Preaching and the Modern Mind*, 55.

These three voices have very different starting points and, quite likely, very different audiences. The main clash in bringing these voices together seems to be between an admittedly African American understanding and one(s) that may be considered more academic. The initial response may be to lean toward more "academic" understandings. This lean, however, accepts two assumptions. First, that the perspective espoused by the Black hermeneutic camp is completely contextualized and, second, that the academic label—on the contrary—is free from contextualization. The perceived academic reading of the prophets must be dislodged from the false moorings of uncontextualized transcendentalism. I argue that these two views should be in conversation and not competition. The goal of defining the prophetic should be to put forth an understanding that is rooted in the biblical record of God's revelation, and that takes seriously the community in which it is being spoken. This language itself sounds much like the Gospel chronicler John, who informs us that the eternal Word of God, the Logos, was made flesh and dwelt among humanity. Or, to borrow from Eugene Peterson, God moved into the neighborhood.

When all three of these scholars are placed in conversation and allowed to complement and critique each other, four key elements arise that can be used to develop a definition of the prophetic.

## Rooted in God

Any proper understanding of the prophetic must, first and foremost, be rooted in God as the initiator of creation and revelation. God creates all that exists *ex nihilo*, from nothing but with a design or plan in mind.[13] God creates humanity in God's own likeness and image. Not leaving creation to chance, God enters into relationship with what God has made desiring communion and fellowship with humanity. All of this is known through revelation—the act of God revealing Godself to humanity. God speaks to and through humanity throughout history to foster this relationship even through flawed humans. No enterprise of understanding of the prophetic can begin without a denial of deism and an affirmation of the fact that God creates and God reveals.

---

13. To quote Niringiye, "He is the one who began all—he created all, out of nothing" (*Church*, 58). Niringiye also points out the plan and desire of God to restore communion with humanity and creation.

Since God is the creator—or architect, as it were—it stands to reason that there is some divine plan, will, or design for humanity and creation. As imperfect beings prone to the lure, power, and control of sin, humans often need to be reminded of God's intention for humanity and creation. God raises up voices and messengers as correctives to remind humanity of how we have missed that vision. These voices remind us what we experience and call reality is neither eternal nor fully factual. The architect holds the true and accurate blueprints and uses prophetic voices to discomfort those who have bought into an alternate version of truth. These voices do not rise up of their own accord, for the calling and vision must come from the creator. It is not enough that something is good or moral. To be truly prophetic, it must originate and emanate from God, the creator. "For prophecy is a sham unless it is experienced as a word of God swooping down on man and converting him into a prophet."[14] However, most prophets were not received well. Many were viewed as heretics or ungodly—maybe even profane considering some of the actions God led them into. A pastor today would be hard-pressed to convince a congregation that God called him to marry a porn star or to name his daughter "Unloved," both of which the book of Hosea pictures.

## Speaks Truth to Power

If the first pillar deals with origin, the second looks to function. Serious attention to the ministry and persons of the biblical prophets reveals a critique of existing power structures that subverted the carrying out of God's concepts of justice, righteousness, and worship.[15] Nearly all of the authors understand that there is a design for human government in which God desires equality and equity for all people. There is also overwhelming agreement among these diverse voices that human government strays from a design of justice, mercy, and equity because human government is always corrupted by sin and power. This corruption positions its systems and ways of being over and against those revealed by God. Eventually, according to Brueggemann, the "royal consciousness" will coopt divine truth leaving people with an inability to face death or symbols that point to realities beyond that of the royal consciousness.[16] Each consciousness is waging

14. Heschel, *Prophets*, xviii.
15. This is Brueggemann's royal consciousness and Black theology's power.
16. Brueggemann, *Prophetic Imagination*, 49.

## Part One: Call

war. The result is a battle between realities, one true and one purporting to be. As Brueggemann puts it, "The backdrop of prophetic preaching is the dispute between two narratives."[17]

This war being raged for the attentiveness and consciousness of humanity is being discussed in theoretical, spiritual, or philosophical language, but make no mistake, the consequences of these narratives play out in the existential realities of human beings. The injustice and violence experienced by the disinherited—to borrow from Howard Thurman[18]—are not imaginary. Chattel slavery, Jim Crow, systemic injustice, and other forms of racism inflicted upon Black bodies by White supremacist ideology and theology are real. While Black theology emphasizes this plight, it is not to the exclusion of the conversation Heschel and Brueggemann engage in. Rather, they are two sides of the same coin. Brueggemann points out that the royal consciousness opposes God, while the tradition of Black preaching (including Black theology) describes how this opposition plays out in the society and academia of modern-day America. The positions are not mutually exclusive. In fact, when they are allowed to speak to each other—and not over each other—they help to fully flesh out the prophetic.

God raises prophets to evoke, form, and reform an alternative community according to God's vision and design. Heschel says that the prophet must, then, reject and condemn the elements of society that God disagrees with. Indeed, the prophet functions as the cry that will speak truth to power unrelentingly. More specifically, the prophet will speak God's truth to corrupted power presenting itself as true.

Jeremiah and Jesus both condemn the temple for not being a place where all nations could come and find God's mercy and justice, for being a place that coopted God's intention and masked God's narrative. The voice of the prophets was always considered subversive, counter-cultural, and at times heretical. The prophetic always has the tendency to sound heretical in a place where the royal consciousness—power—presents a "captive God."[19] Heretical in that the prophetic will need to be a critique of the established order of worship practices—religion and public faith. The captive God of the royal consciousness is a version of God, religion, or worship that has been coopted by power. God is surely discussed and lifted within the oppressive

---

17. Brueggemann, *Practice of Prophetic Imagination*, loc. 227.
18. Thurman, *Jesus and the Disinherited*.
19. Brueggemann, *Prophetic Imagination*, 36.

system, but God is not free to act as God chooses.[20] Rather, this version of God allows the powerful and their ideology to be at ease in its presence because it ultimately serves the empire's purposes. The prophet must, then, be jarring, subversive, imaginative, and abrasive to stir the people out of a lulled sense of being. An abrasive and subversive delivery could easily be interpreted by some as profane, especially in a literal sense of relating to or devoted to that which is not sacred.

## Deals with Heaven and Earth

The underlying issue that all of the scholars are trying to navigate—at least Brueggemann and Heschel—is whether or not the prophetic equals social justice and action. Lesslie Newbigin is helpful in navigating this space. He reminds us that our eschatology should inform our ecclesiology and theology.[21] If we ultimately believe the words of Jesus concerning the kingdom of heaven—that it is both being fulfilled and will be fulfilled—then we cannot forsake the political action required in our society. One cannot enter into honest Christian devotion and action that honors God and relinquish any claim or control over social life. We cannot truly love our neighbor and neglect political and social action that directly impacts the life of that neighbor.

Just as God's concern is over the eternal and the temporary, so is the concern of the prophetic. God's prophet is called at a particular time and tied to a particular moment.[22] The call of that prophet is an intervention by God, and that intervention is not just heavenly or ethereal. Martin-Achard and Re'emi hold, "The God of scriptures does not act in a vague, impersonal manner. His interventions are seen to be with real and factual people and in particular places and times."[23] Heschel adds, "The calling of the prophet may be described as that of an advocate or champion, speaking for those who are too weak to plead their own cause."[24] His language in his chapter on justice very much rings the social justice bell. However, Heschel is clear that prophets don't speak simply for justice but for the pathos of God, the God of justice. Notice, again, the convergence of the streams. Some may argue that the Old Testament prophets were not particularly concerned with

20. It is often "God" that is used to implement or reinforce the oppressive systems.
21. Newbigin, *Signs amid the Rubble*.
22. Martin-Achard and Re'emi, *God's People in Crisis*, 11.
23. Martin-Achard and Re'emi, *God's People in Crisis*, 12.
24. Heschel, *Prophets*, 205.

specific events or causes in their societies; especially the way social justice is viewed today.²⁵ Yet, even those who don't see this as a focus of the prophetic don't deny that the prophets did indeed speak to physical kings, actual false prophets, corrupt courts, and condemn existing social, political, and economic practices, policies, and systems. These social and political acts are not the main agenda or sole focus of the prophets, but this aspect cannot be denied in the prophetic activity as seen in Scripture. Hence, justice cannot be precluded from a biblical understanding of prophetic. This pillar contends that the prophetic must engage heaven and earth. "The biblical prophet heard God speak in the midst of the real historical situation."²⁶ Jeremiah did not prophesy of a theoretical destruction of Jerusalem, but of actual devastating loss.

## Spoken Through Poetry/Music

This last pillar is more about methodology than an actual dictate of the prophetic. Most of the scholars, too, recognize the tendency for the prophetic to engage in poetry and music.²⁷ The poetic is useful because it is imaginative and passionate and energizes the imaginations of the people. Brueggemann believes that the artist or poet is more apt to this work since they are more concerned with imagination than implementation.²⁸ Heschel sees the imaginative gift of poets and artists as ideal for prophetic work.

---

25. Brueggemann, *Practice of Prophetic Imagination*, loc. 72–73.

26. Olan, *Prophetic Faith and the Secular Age*, 7.

27. While the reasons may be somewhat distinct, this consensus cannot be overlooked. Heschel says that the prophet is like a poet/artist who has a "heightened and unified awareness of certain aspects of life" (*Prophets*, 367). He also goes on to say that, biblically, poetry was considered to be divinely inspired (Heschel, *Prophets*, 386–87). Brueggemann is adamant that "the characteristic way of a prophet in Israel is that of poetry and lyric" (*Prophetic Imagination*, 45). He would also later contribute that the prophetic is "subversive verbal probe" that utilizes poetic language of metaphor to critique power and energize hope for justice (*Practice of Prophetic Imagination*, loc. 583). Speaking for the Black music tradition, Cornel West (*Prophesy Deliverance!*, 7) affirms that it is prophetic. Returning specifically to Black preaching, Otis Moss III connects the prophetic to Amos and Isaiah, and the rhythmic cadence (Moss, "Real Big").

28. The reader must also understand, however, that Brueggemann's point here is that the prophet is not a systems-person. They are not the ones to work out the "how" of revolution and rededication. Olan also agrees that the prophets do not have "a blueprint for the ideal political or economic social order" (*Prophetic Faith and the Secular Age*, xiii).

The tradition of Black preaching has long included musicality and poetic language.

This section has maintained, through these scholars, that the prophetic is this sustained battle for the consciousness and imagination of God's people. Poetry and music are extremely affective and imaginative. They engage the cognitive and creative process in both the artists and the audience. If the prophetic is to "cut through the numbness" of the deceptive reality of power to reveal God's narrative, it must be done with passion.[29]

## Summary

I submit, then, that the prophetic is the vocalization of a God-given narrative that wars against the prevalent narrative rooted in power, corruption, and oppression that is often expressed poetically and/or musically. This leads back to the primary question, "Is hip-hop prophetic?" Let's answer this in reverse order, saving the most complicated and first pillar for last.

The musical and poetic nature of hip-hop has been expressed and attested since its genesis. The vast literature on hip-hop nullifies any need for further demonstration. However, not all music/poetry is divinely inspired; it merely checks off this one box. Yes, hip-hop is musical and poetic.

Does hip-hop touch heaven and earth? The harshest critics would agree that it touches or deals with the earth, much like its mother—the blues. Does it, however, touch heaven? James Cone's classic work *The Spirituals and the Blues* answers this directly.[30] He contends that the Spirituals and the blues both flow from the same fount: the Black experience in America. Yet they are inherently positioned against each other. The Spirituals spoke explicitly of God, and the blues spoke explicitly of lived experiences. Culturally, neither accepted the other; they were mutually exclusive to many. The Black church condemned the blues and those who performed it. Cone, however, uncovers the shared genesis of both and urges the reader to receive the blues as a type of "secular spiritual."[31] He explains, "They are secular in the sense that they confine their attention solely to the immediate and affirm the bodily expression of black soul, including its sexual manifestations. They are spirituals because they are impelled by the same search

---

29. Brueggemann, *Prophetic Imagination*, 49.
30. Cone, *Spirituals and the Blues*.
31. Cone, *Spirituals and the Blues*, loc. 1423.

for the truth of black experience."[32] The beauty of the blues, for Cone, was that they were not bothered with the "religious concerns of the church," but they were, in every way, thinking about and talking to God.[33] To bring Cone's language into this conversation, he would have considered the blues profane and prophetic. He doubled down on the connection between the two, insisting they were not mutually exclusive. Rather, neither was a complete picture of Black life without the other. Cone ended the volume by declaring that the contemporary genres of Gospel music and hip-hop are the children of the Spirituals and the blues.[34] Hip-hop, as the daughter of the blues, is indeed looking to heaven and to earth. One need only review the lyrics of some of the most popular artists to see and hear a cry out to God and against the conditions of life.[35]

"Hip-hop artists are often self-proclaimed contemporary prophets, their work constructed of truth-revealing parables and pictures."[36] Imani Perry details that tangled up in the difficult understanding of hip-hop is a subversive message that strikes to the heart of hegemony and White supremacy.[37] For Perry, hip-hop is complicated, but part of its complexity is a critique of oppression. Hip-hop was born in poverty; it "took root in a culture of hardship."[38] Perhaps that particular sociocultural matrix is the rationale behind the consistent railing against systemic issues like racist policing, unjust prison sentences, political corruption, crime, and violence—topics that evoke strong emotional responses. Remember that Heschel called prophecy the voice God lends to the silent agony and plundered poor. In this vein, hip-hop bears "witness to the invisible suffering of the masses."[39] When at its best, the culture reveals the guttural cry of a reality

---

32. *Spirituals and the Blues*, loc. 1423.

33. Cone is not alone in his high regard for the spiritual content of the blues. Spencer says that people in the blues articulate religious worldview in "lore and lyric rather than in scholarly discourse" (*Blues and Evil*, 35). Spencer also calls the blues a "secular religion" and calls the artists "prophets and visionaries" (35).

34. In my estimation, this makes them first cousins, and much more connected and related than the casual observer may understand. Separately Perry also charts the roots of hip-hop to blues and jazz: Perry, *Prophets of the Hood*, 8.

35. See 2Pac, "I Wonder If Heaven Got a Ghetto"; DMX, "Lord Give Me a Sign"; and Grandmaster Flash and the Furious Five, "Message," for examples.

36. Perry, *Prophets of the Hood*, 2.

37. Perry, *Prophets of the Hood*, 104.

38. Dyson, Jay-Z, and Nas, *Know What I Mean?*, 72.

39. Dyson, *Debating Race*, 234.

lived in oppressive and depressing conditions created by an imbalanced and unequitable human system. While hip-hop is not unified or monolithic, it does indeed speak truth to power. "Hip-hop addresses the crisis of urban America and begins to seek spiritual answers connected to Jesus."[40]

But can you say that hip-hop comes from God? While there is violence and vulgarity in hip-hop, there is also consciousness, positivity, and God-talk. As with any culture (cultural group, cultural product, etc.) there are things that can be classified as positive and negative. The fact that hip-hop culture contains sinful or morally deplorable components cannot make it automatically devoid of God's care and voice. The church, as it has been historically practiced by people, is flawed and filled with failure and horror, alongside hope. Yet we do not throw out the church. Neither can we throw out hip-hop culture and assume God's absence from it. To do so is to simultaneously disqualify every human effort and nullify the omnipresence of God. Such sweeping judgment is especially problematic when we condemn hip-hop without close listening, which effectually mutes the reality of agony because of the verbiage of pain. If God speaks through donkeys, fires, children, and flawed humans, God can speak through hip-hop. Hip-hop is one way that God gut checks the church into remembering that things are not alright. God can—and does—speak through hip-hop, both through artists who are devoted and professing Christians carrying explicitly orthodox messages and through those who might not identify as Christian and whose messages don't conform to orthodoxy. God's voice of challenging broken human systems and envisioning alternate possibilities for people to thrive is present in hip-hop. It comes through in questions about God's presence amid suffering. It is apparent in the Christological references embedded in lyrics. It is visible in the ecclesiological imagery artists use to convey "secular" concepts via a shared lexicon of the Black church.

The reality is that our sacred Scriptures contain material that is offensive. Women are called cows and dogs, rape and murder are rampant, power is abused, and we call it sacred (rightly so). Is God done speaking? Was God only concerned about our faith ancestors and their lived realities? Was that the only time period when power and orthodoxy were used to oppress and minoritize opinions that did not prop up empire? Might God be raising up voices today that are unafraid to challenge religious hegemony for the sake of truth and liberation? Perhaps we need to open ourselves to the possibility of the profane and prophetic.

---

40. Hodge, *Soul of Hip Hop*, 591.

Part One: Call

## PROFANE. PROPHETIC.

Before closing this chapter, I want to give a few concrete examples of what has been described above, for your consideration. I pray that you lean in, listen, and respond.

D Smoke is a popular hip-hop artist hailing from Inglewood, California. A few years ago he won a televised hip-hop contest that aired on Netflix, called *Rhythm + Flow*. For his final, and winning, performance, D Smoke set the stage to resemble the Last Supper, but in reverse.[41] The scene opens with twelve people at a table mimicking the famous image but with their backs to the audience as Smoke plays a piano and drops his first verse, laden with locally known references. Smoke irreverently uses the image of communion to discuss betrayal and brag about his skills. The repeated metaphors and similes borrowed from the context of Jesus' meal and betrayal are employed to say something about the nature of the contest itself, namely, that he had friends in the competition but knew they could not be completely trusted. Invoking the image of Jesus, the artist saw himself as the rightful king of the contest. Say what you will, the artist understood that the image and words could convey more than he had the space and time to convey with his own words. In the midst of the song, too, is a hope for his city being better and a nostalgic reminder of the things that make it great.

The one and only Lauryn Hill recorded an unplugged album way back in 2002. Lauryn, using only her guitar and her voice, goes into a near three-minute verse that is a complete verbal assault on the corruption of American government. The song, "The Mystery of Iniquity," describes the rampant duplicity of our systems by describing the minute details of a criminal court proceeding as the representation of how evil works through our systems. She calls it evil and full of iniquity. The song, though, is replete with Christian and biblical language. She charges that this system is not right, but she explicitly calls it Babylon and says that the "son of perdition is the commander in chief." She talks about bribes of "30 talents," being in bondage to "Canaanites," cries for Israel to surrender to Jehovah, and talks about crucifixion and repentance. She ends the onslaught with the refrain that we are "loving a lie; not realizing in Adam all die."[42] Lauryn sees herself as a messenger of God disturbing the comfort of the masses to point out the

---

41. Wrench, *Rhythm + Flow*, "Finale."
42. Hill, "Mystery of Iniquity."

brokenness of the system and the brokenness it is causing. She uses biblical language, not because it is easy but because it is God that has sent her and it is God's vision she is trying to cast.

Big Sean released the album *I Decided.* in 2017. The last track on the album is "Bigger Than Me." The artist is hoping that others in his community realize that there is more to life than the "hood America." He stands against the systems that are trying to tear down his community and his extended family.[43] He comes to the realization that success is not about money and tangible items, but it is an opportunity that God has given him to help make changes in his community. This is bigger than him, and he believes that "God is talking to me telepathic." He even wishes that friends that have died could see him now. Not for his own sake but for the sake of what he is trying to inspire.

These, and other artists, see themselves as part of the vocalization of divine will. They have seen and speak keenly about the brokenness of our society and the ways that brokenness impacts actual bodies, families, and communities. Voices such as these are often located outside of the "church" and engage in language and imagery that may not be liturgical, but it is prophetic.

## BIBLIOGRAPHY

2Pac. "I Wonder If Heaven Got a Ghetto." Track 7 on *R U Still Down? (Remember Me)*. Interscope, 1997.

Big Sean. "Bigger Than Me." Track 14 on *I Decided*. Getting Out Our Dreams (G.O.O.D.)/Def Jam Recordings, 2017.

Brueggemann, Walter. *The Practice of Prophetic Imagination: Preaching an Emancipating Word*. Lanham, MD: Fortress, 2012. Kindle.

———. *The Prophetic Imagination*. Philadelphia: Fortress, 1978.

Cone, James H. *The Spirituals and the Blues: An Interpretation*. Maryknoll, NY: Orbis, 1992. Kindle.

DMX. "Lord Give Me a Sign." Track 15 on *Year of the Dog . . . Again*. Ruff Ryders/Sony, 2006.

Dyson, Michael Eric. *Debating Race: With Michael Eric Dyson*. New York: Basic Civitas, 2007.

———. *Holler If You Hear Me: Searching for Tupac Shakur*. New York: Basic Civitas, 2001.

———. *The Michael Eric Dyson Reader*. New York: Basic Civitas, 2004. http://www.aspresolver.com/aspresolver.asp?BLTC;S17209.

---

43. In the lyrics Big Sean says that everyone in his community is like a "distant cousin."

## Part One: Call

Dyson, Michael Eric, Jay-Z, and Nas. *Know What I Mean? Reflections on Hip-Hop*. New York: Basic Civitas, 2007.
Forsyth, Peter T. *Positive Preaching and the Modern Mind*. Grand Rapids: Eerdmans, 1964.
Grandmaster Flash and the Furious Five. "The Message." Track 7 on *The Message*. Sugar Hill, 1982.
Heschel, Abraham J. *The Prophets*. New York: Harper & Row, 1962.
Hill, Lauryn. "The Mystery of Iniquity." Track 2, disc 2, on *MTV Unplugged No. 2.0*. Columbia Records, 2002.
Hodge, Daniel White. *The Soul of Hip Hop: Rims, Timbs and a Cultural Theology*. Downers Grove, IL: InterVarsity, 2010.
Martin-Achard, Robert, and S. Paul Re'emi. *God's People in Crisis: A Commentary on the Books of Amos and Lamentations*. Grand Rapids: Eerdmans, 1984.
McMickle, Marvin Andrew. *Where Have All the Prophets Gone? Reclaiming Prophetic Preaching in America*. Cleveland: Pilgrim, 2006. Kindle.
Moss, Otis, III. "Real Big: The Hip-Hop Pastor as Postmodern Prophet." In *The Gospel Remix: Reaching the Hip-Hop Generation*, edited by Ralph C. Watkins. Valley Forge, PA: Judson, 2007. Kindle.
Moyd, Olin P. *The Sacred Art: Preaching and Theology in the African American Tradition*. Valley Forge, PA: Judson, 1995.
Newbigin, Lesslie. *Signs amid the Rubble: The Purposes of God in Human History*. Edited by Geoffrey Wainwright. Grand Rapids: Eerdmans, 2003.
Niringiye, David Zac. *The Church: God's Pilgrim People*. Downers Grove, IL: InterVarsity, 2015.
Olan, Levi A. *Prophetic Faith and the Secular Age*. Dallas: Institute for Jewish Studies, 1982.
Perry, Imani. *Prophets of the Hood: Politics and Poetics in Hip Hop*. Durham, NC: Duke University Press, 2004.
Rose, Tricia. *Black Noise: Rap Music and Black Culture in Contemporary America*. Hanover, NH: University Press of New England, 1994. Kindle.
Smith, Theophus H. *Conjuring Culture: Biblical Formations of Black America*. New York: Oxford University Press, 1994.
Spencer, Jon Michael. *Blues and Evil*. Knoxville: University of Tennessee Press, 1993.
Thurman, Howard. *Jesus and the Disinherited*. Repr., Boston: Beacon, 1996.
Watkins, Ralph Basui. *Hip-Hop Redemption: Finding God in the Rhythm and the Rhyme*. Grand Rapids: Baker Academic, 2011.
West, Cornel. *Prophesy Deliverance! An Afro-American Revolutionary Christianity*. Anniversary ed. Philadelphia: Westminster, 2002.
Wrench, Sam, dir. *Rhythm + Flow*. "Finale." Season 1, episode 10, aired Oct. 23, 2019, on Netflix.

# 2

## Lyrical Location

*Hip-Hop Artists as Patriots?*

### Alex Sosler

A man, I thought, must be judged by how willingly and meaningfully he can be present where he is, by how fully he can make himself at home in his part of the world. I began to want desperately to learn to belong to my place.
—Wendell Berry

I love America more than any other country in the world, and, exactly for this reason, I insist on the right to criticize her perpetually.
—James Baldwin, *Notes of a Native Son*

What does it mean to love a place? Most hip-hop artists have a located presence and are happy to represent their neighborhood. Jay-Z represents New York in "Empire State of Mind." Tupac moved around but settled with a West Coast identity in "California Love." Drake runs "through the 6

## Part One: Call

(Toronto) with his woes."[1] In "Till I Die," Machine Gun Kelly announces, "I'm from The Land (Cleveland) till I die." As theologian Daniel White Hodge indicates, "Space and place are fundamental elements for hip hop. Street names, area codes and city names provide the hip hop community meaning, identity and community in an environment that has vastly left them unknown."[2] There's a loyalty to place that's primal in hip-hop.

Early on in hip-hop's history, "true" hip-hop came from New York. But even then, the representation of place was borough-specific—the Bronx vs. Queens. Then, the West Coast got involved. As Easy Mo Bee has said, "Hip-hop has always been a sport of competition"[3]—whether it be a fight within the New York City boroughs or the West Coast–East Coast beef. Another emerging region got involved in the 1995 Source Awards in New York City. OutKast received the award for best new rap group. In response, the New York crowd booed them. After some pleasantries and Southern charm, André 3000 took the mic. "I'm tired of folks, you know what I'm saying, close-minded folks, you know what I'm saying. We got a demo tape and don't nobody want to hear it, but it's like the South got something to say. That's all I'm gonna say."[4] Hip-hop history has been a continual opening up of the canon to outsiders and new sounds emerging from different locations. Today, Toronto rapper Drake is often at the top of the charts. Hip-hop can come from anywhere, but there is a strong sense of place and solidarity among hip-hop artists.

Hip-hop has two impulses in regard to place: a love for place by representing your neighborhood and a critique of American structures that keep those neighborhoods impoverished. This chapter will start with the briefest of the histories of land and space in the African American experience. In essence, theirs is a story of perpetual exile. They have the most to critique. However, they also appreciate their place. These two realities—love and critique—are not in competition. They love their place, and they've earned a right to critique it. Hip-hop music shows a way of cultural engagement that incorporates the best elements of optimism and pessimism and, therefore, can teach us how to better live in our own neighborhoods. I will close with a close read of "This Is America" by Childish Gambino, which I will argue is a critique of place that stems from love.

1. Drake, "Know Yourself."
2. Hodge, *Soul of Hip Hop*, 106.
3. Abrams, *Come Up*, 154.
4. André 3000 in Brasch, "How André 3000's Speech."

## THE STORY OF PLACE IN BLACK LIFE

The story of land in America at large has been a story of desecration. From the displacement of indigenous people to the slave trade to industrial destruction, America has a bad track record of caring for and stewarding land. The story of black Americans finds its place within this story of desecration. They have sought a home, sought citizenship, and sought rights that were often denied. They desired roots, but they were often uprooted.

## The Slave Trade

The story of African Americans starts in Africa and their displacement from their land. Robbed of homeland and stripped of heritage, they were brought from the shores of Africa to the shores of America to be commodified, sold, and enslaved.

Yale theologian Willie James Jennings references the account of the Portuguese chronicler Zurara.[5] He argues that the foreign powers reconfigured space and bodies, land, and personhood in the colonial world. He writes of Zurara, "He stands now between bodies and land, and he adjudicates, identifies, determines."[6] That is, the ones with power do not recognize the placedness of bodies but hold themselves as determiners of identity. People became no longer tied or rooted in and to a place but identified by their skin color. Jennings goes on, "Zurara is capturing the twin operations of discovery and consumption. With those twin operations, four things are happening at the same time: first, people are being seized (stolen); second, land is being seized (stolen); third, people are being stripped from their space, their place; and fourth Europeans are describing themselves and these Africans at the same time."[7] As a chronicler, Zurara holds the power to determine and describe. He does not have to listen, but he has the power to adjudicate.

As such, Willie James Jennings calls this journey to the New World a reverse pilgrimage.[8] On holy pilgrimages, the pilgrim is dependent on the kindness and hospitality of others for sustenance and shelter. They search for home and welcome. "But the march of black flesh in bonds to the sea

---

5. Jennings, *Christian Imagination*, 24.
6. Jennings, *Christian Imagination*, 24.
7. Jennings, *Christian Imagination*, 24.
8. Jennings, *Christian Imagination*, 174.

mocked that journey through reversal," Jennings writes. "The march of slaves, greedily hurried black bodies, toward death-filled ports demonically mimicked the divine banishment of the first family from the garden."[9] Africans go from safety to danger. There is no return home. Rather than welcome, they are exploited.

Black Americans' search for rootedness starts with being uprooted and, in many cases, having no place or cultural memory to call home. In some ways, the appeal of the Zulu Nation of Afrika Bambaataa makes sense. Many had no nation to call home. They had no heritage to which to point. They had no common ancestry. They had no tradition. It was lost. The Zulu Nation provides an identity marker and a sense of unity for black Americans.

## Great Migration

The search for place has another narrative that results in uprootedness for black Americans. Faced with threats, lack of opportunity, and the promise of freedom, black Southerners fled the outright racism of the South to a hopeful northern promised land. It came to be known as the Great Migration. From 1915 to 1970, "some six million black southerners left the land of their forefathers and fanned out across the country for an uncertain existence in nearly every other corner of America."[10] At the start, 10 percent of black Americans lived outside the South. By its end, nearly half of the black population lived outside the South.[11] These migrants weren't immigrants in the traditional sense, but they sought the citizenship that was denied them in the South. They were not treated as citizens by their own neighbors. Those responsible for the stewardship of the land before the country was founded ended up being rejected by the land they cultivated. These black Americans searched for freedom, for something better. But fleeing the abject racism of the South, they were welcomed by the more subtle, more institutionalized racism of the North.

The author bell hooks describes her own migration as a conflict of values. She writes, "Leaving the agrarian past meant leaving cultures of belonging and community wherein resources were shared for a culture of liberal individualism. There is very little published work that looks at the

9. Jennings, *Christian Imagination*, 174.
10. Wilkerson, *Warmth of Other Suns*, 9.
11. As documented in Wilkerson, *Warmth of Other Suns*, 10.

psychological turmoil black folks faced as they made serious geographical change that brought with them new psychological demands."[12] She goes on to describe the material and psychological impact. "Black folks wanted to be free from the overt racial harassment that was a constant in southern life and they wanted access to material goods—to a level of material well-being that was not available in the agrarian south where white folks limited access to the spheres of economic power," hooks notes. "Of course, they found that life in the north had its own perverse hardships, that racism was just as virulent there, that it was much harder for black people to become landowners. Without the space to grow food, to commune with nature, or to mediate the starkness of poverty with the splendor of nature, black people experienced profound depression."[13] The Great Migration's hope of freedom, land, and recognition brought many benefits to the black population. They did not have to sit separately at counters or buses. They did not have to fear vigilante violence with no hope for justice in courts. However, the subtle forms of racism created a further sense of exile. The move did not come with a welcome sign.

## Urbanization

By and large, the Great Migration was to cities. The next stop on the historic reverse pilgrimage started with the hope and promise of freedom and protection of the law. Black Americans found it, but they encountered a more secret hideousness than Jim Crow. Through policies like redlining, the search for home didn't end in the North. They went seeking a home, but mortgage companies wouldn't give them one.[14] The anarchy of individual violence of the South moved to the institutionalized injustice of the North. Whether lack of access to mortgages or Robert Moses policies that paved over black neighborhoods to make way for highways, black Americans found themselves consistently rejected. "Blockbusting" was a further practice where real estate agents paid black people to walk around neighborhoods to spook white people to sell their properties on the cheap. Because, of course, when black people move into the neighborhood, home prices plummet. Exiled from community, from their heritage of the South, from

    12. hooks, *Belonging*, 22.

    13. hooks, *Belonging*, 38.

    14. Buying homes on "contract" in Chicago is but one example. See Coates, "Case for Reparations."

nature, they found themselves in urban spaces with still no place to call home.

A product of the Great Migration, novelist Richard Wright comments on his creation of Bigger Thomas, the main character in his *Native Son*. He describes the black consciousness with a "wild and intense longing (wild and intense because it was suppressed!) to belong, to be identified, to feel that they were alive as other people were, to be caught up forgetfully and exultingly in the swing of events, to feel the clean, deep, organic satisfaction of doing a job in common with others."[15] America hasn't yet realized the missed ideal that many black men and women experience.

In the closing speech to his trial, Bigger's lawyer, Max, describes the colonialist mindset to conquer, "but in conquering others, they *used* others, used their lives.... Lives were tools and weapons to be wielded against a hostile land and climate."[16] Urbanization brought the mechanization of life. The industrial revolution that made urbanization desirable furthered the slave instinct and made economic independence impossible. As Grandmaster Flash poetically raps in his "The Message," the urban environment feels like a jungle. It makes me wonder sometimes how black Americans keep from going under.

A psychological dimension comes from the rootlessness of generations that they have little control over. White mobility is the ideal in modernity, but for a long time, black Americans have experienced forced mobility. For me, the most piercing line from Ta-Nehesi Coates's 2014 article "The Case for Reparations" is "Indeed, in America there is a strange and powerful belief that if you stab a black person 10 times, the bleeding stops and the healing begins the moment the assailant drops the knife."[17] The bleeding continues. Americans—black and white—are continually disconnected from place and, therefore, disconnected from land and one another.

## ARE HIP-HOP ARTISTS PATRIOTS?

I document this concise history to show that black Americans have every right to critique their place. It seems like they would be the last population to be patriots.[18] They have little reason to love their place. Yet, they remain

---

15. Wright, "How Bigger Was Born," in *Native Son*, 440.
16. Wright, *Native Son*, 389.
17. Coates, "Case for Reparations."
18. For a fuller discussion of patriotism, see MacIntyre, *Is Patriotism a Virtue?*

provincial, which is a term that can be distinguished, but I'll equate it with patriot. The poet J. C. Scharl describes provincialism this way: "To be provincial is simply to say that you love something deeply, that you believe in the loveliness, or the potential loveliness, of a particular place and its particular ways."[19] Hip-hop artists are provincialists (or patriots) in that they see the potential loveliness of their place even if they haven't lived that experience. As Kimberly Ruffin describes black eco-literary authors, I want to describe the best rappers, "whose imaginations are not stimuli of oppression but whose intellectual vibrancy is capable of negotiating domination and imaginative work outside of oppression's bounds."[20]

In an essay titled "The Flag of the World," Catholic theologian and fiction writer G. K. Chesterton provides commentary on what makes a place great. He corrects a common misinterpretation of optimism and pessimism: "Upon the whole, I came to the conclusion that the optimist thought everything good except the pessimist, and that the pessimist thought everything bad, except himself."[21] He thinks this popular understanding is mistaken. Man is not in some objective position to critique. Rather, "a man belongs to this world before he begins to ask if it is nice to belong to it. . . . To put shortly what seems the essential matter, he has a loyalty long before he has any admiration."[22] Black Americans—perhaps more than white Americans—love America not for a reason but because they are rightful patriots. Their love is bound and loyal. Therefore, we can look to hip-hop artists as rightful and charitable critics of our place.

I want to explore this idea of patriotism a bit further. America, as typically described, is motivated by ideals. Ideals can shape particular behavior but not settled conduct. The patriot ideal is to be of such a character that it is one's conduct. And for that to happen, it needs particulars, not principles. As the agrarian writer Wendell Berry describes a loyalist, "he selflessly respected and intimately felt rather than by general principles telling him what he ought to feel."[23] Berry goes on to explain these dynamics in the Civil War. "In order to go with your people it is necessary to *have* a people with whom you identify and to whom you feel that you belong. To have a people in this sense you must have a place in which you and they

19. Scharl, "Home Is Where One Starts From."
20. Ruffin, *Black on Earth*, 16.
21. Chesterton, *Orthodoxy*, 65.
22. Chesterton, *Orthodoxy*, 65.
23. Berry, *Need to Be Whole*, 199.

have lived together for generations, and to which you mutually feel that you belong. . . . In such a circumstance, people's attention will have begun to shift from that which belongs to them and to that to which they belong."[24] It could be that those from urban environments where hip-hop emerges are one of the few communities left where one can truly "have a people." It's no wonder that hip-hop artists tend to be loyal to their place. Upper-class mobility has no ties. Rather than loving a place, we've become a machine civilization where people are tools to move rather than image bearers to care for in place.

This liberal moral order, which Jennings calls the "whiteness," or you could call modernity, leads to a placelessness. It encourages impartial actors who are citizens of nowhere with no bias. But care necessitates particulars. As Wendell Berry comments, "The removal from the land of so many people removes from the land also those people's love, care, skill, and work. . . . But mere arithmetic tells us that if so many people who have the most direct and practical reasons to love the country are removed from the country, then the country will be less loved. There will be a great reduction of patriotism, in the true sense of the world."[25] These urban hip-hop artists can lead the way to a localism that loves and nurtures its communities. The hip-hop artist Paul Wall says that the best hip-hop is local. "To me, local is always better. . . . The top artists, they're Local as f***, for the most part."[26] There's something about Snoop Dogg, for example, that is Long Beach, or Lil' Wayne that is New Orleans. They carry a culture with them. They are authentically placed.

## THIS IS AMERICA

Toward the end of a great film called *The Last Black Man in San Francisco*, the lead character, Jimmie Fails III, sits on a bus rejected and dejected from the place that he loves. He overhears two uppity girls saying that they hate San Francisco. They think San Francisco is a dead city, and they want to move someplace cool—like Los Angeles. "Excuse me," Jimmie interrupts, "Do you love it? . . . You don't get to hate it unless you love it."[27] Hip-hop artists have earned the right to be heard because they love America. That may

24. Berry, *Need to Be Whole*, 203.
25. Berry, *Need to Be Whole*, 11.
26. Paul Wall in Abrams, *Come Up*, 289.
27. Talbot, *Last Black Man*.

sound superficial and juvenile. (Aren't hip-hop artists America's biggest critics? And aren't politicians and those in power typically most critical of hip-hop artists for corrupting America's youth? Didn't N.W.A. say "F*** the police"?) Point taken. But my argument is that they critique America as patriots. They see the potential loveliness of this place, the ideals we say we espouse, and they help us see where America fails.

As a case study, I employ Childish Gambino's "This Is America." With such a title, Childish Gambino picks up the legacy of the twentieth-century poet and social activist Langston Hughes. Hughes begins an article with these words: "This is my land, America. Naturally, I love it—it is home—and I am vitally concerned about its *mores*, its democracy, and its well-being."[28] His desire is to see America with unprejudiced eyes. But he notices something. Those who arrive on America's shores who cannot even speak English have greater freedoms than he does, even though his history is deeper in this place. Immigrants can travel freely, work at skilled jobs, vote, and purchase tickets for various events. He cannot. He critiques his place, but he also notes that he lives in a land where he can write his critique. He can call America to its higher ideals. Too often, blanket statements are used where carefulness is needed.

Poetically, he pens these thoughts in a poem called "Let America Be America Again," where he has a refrain of "America was never America to me." He identifies the oppressed—whether the "red man" whose land was stolen or the "young man" who gets involved in the rat race of industry's "more," or the black man who's lynched.[29] In all of these cases, the dream of America has never been. His aching words long for the America that has never been. Hughes's sentiments are akin to James Baldwin's words in the epigraph of this chapter: "I love America more than any other country in the world, and, exactly for this reason, I insist on the right to criticize her perpetually."[30] Childish Gambino picks up this legacy of love and criticism.

When the video for "This Is America" first came out, it exploded on the internet scene with 7.2 million views in one day.[31] As an artist, Childish Gambino does what James Cone says artists do: "force us to see things we do not want to look at because they make us uncomfortable with ourselves

---

28. Hughes, "Langston Hughes: My America," para. 1.

29. Hughes, "Let America Be America Again," in *Collected Poems of Langston Hughes*, 189.

30. Baldwin, *Notes of a Native Son*, 9.

31. White, "'This Is America' Is the New Minstrel Show."

and the world we have created."[32] The video begins with a shirtless Childish Gambino overlaid with bright lyrics about wanting to party and wanting money. Then, the music mixes with some slow and lower tones, creating an eerie dissonance as Childish Gambino starts to dance. He wistfully moves his body over to a blindfolded man and executes him in the back of the head. The stance he takes as he pulls the trigger is like a common minstrel trope. A minstrel was typically a white person who donned blackface to entertain the audience. The bright music fades away to a southern trap beat and the title of the song is announced, "This is America"—subtly hinting that blacks are exploited for entertainment, just like minstrels did. The trap music is interlaced with a South African choir, which creates further dissonance, merging the sacred and secular, bright and communal versus pared down and heavy. The music video shows the same: young black children smiling and doing "viral" dance moves while robberies, gun violence, and police brutality are out of focus in the background. Popular culture likes the positive things that we can exploit from the black and urban communities; we just ignore the pain and violence from which it emerges. Childish Gambino is foregrounding this dissonance and forces viewers to see it. As Claude Atcho comments on Ralph Ellison's *Invisible Man*, so Childish Gambino features it in his video. "Black people are visible only within the confines of a commodified existence. Representatives of every slice of society gaze upon Invisible as a means to an end, a human prop for fetishized entertainment and a muzzled voice for proclaiming that the absence of equality is due to the absence of Black responsibility."[33] The choir refrain of the song is "Get yo money (black man)."[34] If only black people worked harder, focused on the positive, and smiled and danced a little, they could get ahead. Meanwhile, chaos is in their street.

Unfortunately, the black body's performance has always been under scrutiny in America. Willie James Jennings comments on this underlying force. "'The owner's standard of measure'—this sublime phrase hints at the slave masters' complex practices of slave evaluation tied to one single goal: utility. The lens through which the masters looked at the slaves and taught slaveholding society to look at black flesh was one of use-value. How useful is black flesh? Was the black body docile, friendly, loving, industrious, and positive? Or was it malicious, rebellious, deceitful, lazy, and haughty?

32. Cone, *Cross and the Lynching Tree*, 117.
33. Atcho, *Reading Black Books*, 13.
34. Childish Gambino, "This Is America."

I am careful to say 'body' and not 'person,' because black flesh was first a commodity."[35] This commodification haunts American consciousness and, as Childish Gambino shows, haunts black America.

The video ends in black, and then the screen pans up to a new scene picturing the back of Childish Gambino running. The camera then switches perspectives to the front of the running character. Faintly, you see his eyes. They are filled with fear as a mob runs after him. As Howard Thurman writes, "Fear is one of the most persistent hounds of hell that dog the footsteps of the poor, the dispossessed, the disinherited."[36] I'm confronted with the question that he may be asking: "Do you see me?" It's a moment Karl Barth describes. "It is a great and solemn and incomparable moment" when two persons "look themselves in the eye and discover one another." This moment of seeing "is in some sense the root of all humanity without which the rest is impossible."[37] "This Is America" invites us to look into the reality of black America through black eyes. It is hard and difficult, but we ought not look away.

Childish Gambino is one voice in many hip-hop artists that critique America. But sometimes, the grotesque is needed to shock the majority culture to take notice. Hip-hop artists are not content to present the world kitsch (which is so often a critique of theological art). Kitsch is a cheap substitute for the hard work of nuance and understanding. In the words of Calvin Seerveld, "Kitsch oversimplifies emotional nuances and reduces aesthetically sensitive life to a one-track, predictable, pseudo-transcendent satisfaction."[38] These critiques of place are anything but kitsch.

## A REDEMPTIVE VISION OF PLACE

In the closing pages of *The Christian Imagination*, Willie James Jennings paints a way forward between space and belonging. Rather than a commodified people based on commodified space, we need a new way to imagine people and place. He writes, "The space of communion is always ready to appear where the people of God reach down to join the land and reach out to join those around them, their near and distant neighbors."[39] In our

---

35. Jennings, *Christian Imagination*, 242.
36. Thurman, *Jesus and the Disinherited*, 26.
37. Barth, *Church Dogmatics* 3/2:251–52.
38. Seerveld, *Rainbows for a Fallen World*, 66.
39. Jennings, *Christian Imagination*, 286.

## Part One: Call

global and technological world one way of bringing near distant neighbors is through things like art and music videos. We need virtual eyes to see reconciliation when we are so divided and separate.

A recent critique of hip-hop is the continued impoverishment of inner-city neighborhoods from where hip-hop emerges. Money has flowed into these communities through hip-hop, yet those same communities are floundering. I hope the brief history shows that it's not all hip-hop's fault. There are some systematic and institutional challenges. The bleeding that results from the proverbial stab wounds still flows. Yet I think it's a fair challenge for hip-hop artists to invest in infrastructure and policy to enrich their neighborhoods. One example from a previous age is worth sharing.

Mahalia Jackson was a product of the Great Migration. Born in New Orleans in 1911, her family moved to Chicago, Illinois, in her adolescence. Blessed with a beautiful voice, she rose to prominence in American culture. As Alice Randall notes in an article in Southern Foodways titled "Glori-fried and Glori-fied," "Mahalia Jackson was the first, and arguably the most significant, black female superstar of the twentieth century."[40] She used this fame in the church and encouraged the gospel blues in the church, but her influence also surpassed the church walls. Famously, she marched along Martin Luther King Jr. and became an activist in other political causes. But her influence was also local. She sang, "I'm going to feast with the Rose of Sharon," announcing an integrated table where she will eat in the kingdom of God. She would lay down her burden for the feast. She wasn't going to be a maidservant or preparer at this feast. She was a participant. This future reality compelled her into local care.

Mahalia Jackson opened a fried chicken franchise. Randall posits, "By lending her name and her image to the fried chicken enterprise, Jackson was trying to put a choir robe over a maid's uniform before stripping them both off in favor of a knit business suit. She entered respectability through the shaming kitchen door, kicking the door down as she stepped."[41] These black-owned businesses employed black people and offered employees paid time off, a dignified wage, and other benefits. It was a taste of the kingdom, feasting with the Rose of Sharon in miniscule. Embedded in the black communities they served, "She went into the chicken business to help others make money, and quite possibly to redeem kitchen work, to transform it from a private hell into a public and pride-filled business defined by stock

---

40. Randall, "Glori-fried and Glori-fied."
41. Randall, "Glori-fried and Glori-fied."

and dividends rather than slaps, insults, toting privileges, and rape. Mahalia Jackson understood the power of food. She claimed as her greatest pleasure and entertainment feeding people in her home. She knew food to be a personal pleasure, a spiritual necessity, and a political statement."[42] The way of investment in communities may start with food.

But as Randall notes, the goal is not merely to feed urban communities. With black ownership and concern for human dignity, Jackson offered these communities a different imagination. She gave them a vision of life. Efforts like Killer Mike starting black businesses and banks in Atlanta carry on Jackson's legacy.

## CONCLUSION

The Christian identity is one of sojourner, stranger, and resident aliens. Peter addresses the church as sojourners and exiles. In Heb 11, the author of Hebrews describes the faithful of the past never obtaining the promises that God made. In line with these identities, hip-hop artists understand being weary travelers. Ralph Basui Watkins notes that historic African American communities have focused on the Exodus and Moses narratives for survival in a foreign land. However, he goes on to suggest that the Joseph narrative may be a more apt picture for survival in today's America as black people, like Joseph in captivity, make a home in a foreign place.[43] In essence, anywhere can become a "Land of Promise."[44] In many ways, the story of black Americans has been this story: stubbornly clinging to and cultivating a Land of Promise as many try to strip or deny their Promise. This posture doesn't lead to pessimism or optimism. It is not constant critique in hip-hop. But neither can you look at their history with unrelenting optimism. The dream is still in the future.

As Chesterton realizes in his reflections on place and patriotism, so hip-hop artists can display the same longing: "I had found this hole in the world: the fact that one must somehow find a way of loving the world without trusting it; somehow one must love the world without being worldly."[45] Hip-hop artists aren't in danger of trusting the promise of America, yet they are the ones who are pushing us forward to it. This is life in between

---

42. Randall, "Glori-fried and Glori-fied."
43. Watkins, *Hip-Hop Redemption*, 58.
44. See Murray, *Hero and the Blues*, 61.
45. Chesterton, *Orthodoxy*, 79.

## Part One: Call

the times—between Christ's coming and second coming. The fullness of this vision lies within Christianity. There's a homesick even in our homes. Hope pulls us to the future.

Communion is the goal, and communion starts in place. It starts by reimagining place and bodies in place. It will require the transgression of boundaries, space, and neighborhoods. In order to live faithfully in place, we need to love it. This love will require commitments to place—even in unexpected places, blocks, and area codes.

## BIBLIOGRAPHY

Abrams, Jonathon. *The Come Up: An Oral History of the Rise of Hip Hop*. New York: Crown, 2022.

Atcho, Claude. *Reading Black Books: How African American Literature Can Make Our Faith More Whole and Just*. Grand Rapids: Brazos, 2022.

Baldwin, James. *Notes of a Native Son*. Boston: Beacon, 2012.

Barth, Karl. *Church Dogmatics*. 3/2: *The Doctrine of Creation*. Edited by G. W. Bromiley and T. F. Torrance; translated by H. Knight et al. New York: T&T Clark, 2009.

Berry, Wendell. *The Need to Be Whole: Patriotism and the History of Prejudice*. Berkeley: Shoemaker & Company, 2022.

Brasch, Ben. "How André 3000's 'The South Got Something to Say' Speech Changed Hip-Hop." *Washington Post*, Aug. 7, 2023. https://www.washingtonpost.com/history/2023/08/07/hip-hop-andre-3000-southern-rap/.

Chesterton, G. K. *Orthodoxy*. New York: Image, 2014.

Childish Gambino. "This Is America (Official Video)." YouTube video, 6:05, Jan. 5, 2018. https://www.youtube.com/watch?v=VYOjWnS4cMY.

Coates, Ta-Nehesi. "The Case for Reparations." *Atlantic*, June 2014. https://www.theatlantic.com/magazine/archive/2014/06/the-case-for-reparations/361631/.

Cone, James. *The Cross and the Lynching Tree*. Maryknoll, NY: Orbis, 2013.

Drake. "Know Yourself." Track 4 on *If You're Reading This, It's Too Late*. Universal Music Group, 2015.

Hodge, Daniel White. *Hip Hop's Hostile Gospel: A Post-Soul Theological Exploration*. Leiden: Brill, 2017.

hooks, bell. *Belonging: A Culture of Place*. New York: Routledge, 2008.

Hughes, Langston. *The Collected Poems of Langston Hughes*. New York: Knopf, 1994.

———. "Langston Hughes: My America." *Church Life Journal*, Jan. 16, 2023. https://churchlifejournal.nd.edu/articles/langston-hughes-my-america/.

Jennings, Willie James. *The Christian Imagination: Theology and the Origins of Race*. New Haven: Yale University Press, 2011.

MacIntyre, Alasdair. *Is Patriotism a Virtue? The Lindley Lecture*. Lawrence: University of Kansas, 1984.

Murray, Albert. *The Hero and the Blues*. New York: Knopf Doubleday, 1992.

Randall, Alice. "Glori-fried and Glori-fied: Mahalia Jackson's Chicken." *Gravy*, Feb. 3, 2016. https://www.southernfoodways.org/glori-fried-and-glori-fied-mahalia-jacksons-chicken/.

Ruffin, Kimberly. *Black on Earth: African American Ecoliterary Traditions*. Athens: University of Georgia Press, 2010.

Scharl, J. C. "Home Is Where One Starts From." *Comment Magazine,* Nov. 23, 2023. https://comment.org/home-is-where-one-starts-from/.

Seerveld, Calvin. *Rainbows for a Fallen World*. Toronto: Toronto Tuppence, 1995.

Talbot, Joe, dir. *The Last Black Man in San Francisco*. New York: A24, 2019.

Thurman, Howard. *Jesus and the Disinherited*. Boston: Beacon, 1996.

Watkins, Ralph Basui. *Hip-Hop Redemption: Finding God in the Rhythm and the Rhyme*. Grand Rapids: Baker Academic, 2011.

White, Armond. "'This Is America' Is the New Minstrel Show." *National Review,* May 7, 2018. https://www.nationalreview.com/2018/05/donald-glover-this-is-america-video-political-paranoia/.

Wilkerson, Isabel. *The Warmth of Other Suns: The Epic Story of America's Great Migration*. New York: Vintage, 2011.

Wright, Richard. *Native Son*. New York: Harpers, 2005.

# Part Two

Response

# 3

# Eschatological Flow

*Theology, Temporality, and Rhythm in OutKast's "Rosa Parks"*

C. M. HOWELL

## INTRODUCTION

MUSIC HAS LONG BEEN singled out among the arts for its unique relationship to time. Music *moves* by a certain freedom. It is not wholly chaotic, having no meter or rhythm; but it is also not determined, as if it fell under the strictly causal processes of nature. Music has its own time that falls in accord with its own particularities. This means that, alongside offering a different perspective on temporality itself, different styles of music bring forth time in unique ways.

An important aspect of what makes hip-hop unique, what makes it stand out from other cultural expressions, is the way it moves. Hip-hop's movement is apparent in each of Afrika Bambaataa's categories of hip-hop's aesthetic:[1] in graffiti, the letters and semiotics have a distinctive movement, almost dancing on their urban canvases; break dancing is explicitly a new

---

1. Chang, "Introduction: Hip-Hop Arts," x; cf. Rose, *Black Noise*, 38–39.

way to move during the "breaks" of songs;[2] those very breaks are produced by the innovative movement of records on the turntable of DJs; and MCs, more the focus of this chapter, are judged by the way they move over the beat and free from linguistic standards. This last category is so prevalent, that some have argued for augmenting Bambaataa's four-fold description by adding freestyling as a category on its own.[3]

The theological resonances of such a movement have not gone unnoticed. Ralph Basui Watkins, for example, describes the movement of hip-hop as a quest for liberation that erupts through the artistic customs of the black community.[4] James Perkinson sees the movement of the MC's flow as imitating the "movement of a narrative" leading to some ethical end.[5] The question of ethics aside, simply the dynamics of movement point forward to some other time, or even, some other way to exist. From a theological perspective, the inherent temporality of movement places it quite naturally into conversation with eschatology. Temporality most generally indicates that there is a direction to experience in the world, and eschatology concerns the "end" of time. The abundance of rhythm in hip-hop allows the world to feel itself moving to that end. From a theology of hip-hop perspective, eschatology is uniquely viewed through Watkins's lens of a quest for liberation. The apostle John wrote Revelation in persecution and suffering, one of the most formidable books of the biblical canon to deal with the subject of time.

OutKast will serve as the basis for such an eschatological exploration, for several reasons. William Jelani Cobb asserts that the emergence of Southern hip-hop can be "placed almost squarely on the shoulders of OutKast."[6] Their 1998 album *Aquemini* is regularly heralded as the greatest of Southern hip-hop's expressions, as it went platinum only two months after its release and sold an additional million copies by the next year. David Banner adds that the "honesty" of Southern rap affords that the same person in a single song "can talk about God and talk about the club in the same sentence."[7] André 3000 alludes to something similar in the first verse of the album saying, from the critics' perspective, "y'all be gospel rapping."

2. Perkinson, "Underneath the MC's Wit," 14.
3. Watkins, *Hip-Hop Redemption*, 16–17.
4. Watkins, *Hip-Hop Redemption*, 32.
5. Perkinson, "Underneath the MC's Wit," 14.
6. Cobb, *To the Break of Dawn*, 74.
7. Banner, foreword to *Chicken-Fried Soul*, 7.

The track "Rosa Parks" was the most successful of the album, reaching number 55 on the *Billboard* Hot 100 chart, and receiving a Grammy nomination in 1999. It has been singled out on the album as a particularly powerful example of the group's "distinctive style."[8] In this chapter, the track is fitting for an analysis of flow's temporality because its somewhat simplistic beat highlights the lyrical dynamics that float above it. The track is also composed of original music, lacking any samples, and enacts "breaks" in the music at unpredictable, but significant, places. As discussed below, these breaks increase the intensity of the listening experiencing, forcing attention to shifts in the track's temporal shape. "Rosa Parks" brings this dimension to the forefront, making the track well suited for an eschatological reading of hip-hop's time.[9]

In light of the focus on temporality, a sustained lyrical analysis will be largely absent from what follows. This is not because such studies are not warranted, but because by bracketing off the word, the musicological image can better appear.[10] I am interested in how "Rosa Parks" is temporally experienced, how it is heard, and how the rhythm moves on its own and as a basis for linguistic meaning. The question I want to raise narrows in on the particularities of hip-hop's temporality. It is not to generally "enquire as to the ways in which music can benefit theology,"[11] but, rather, the more specific question: how does hip-hop influence a perception of theology? Or, more specifically, a perception of eschatology?

To such an aim, a theological evaluation of music and temporality will provide the initial working concepts to gain a foothold in the discussion. This evaluation will then be augmented by the aesthetically specific concepts of "flow" and "cadence." The weight of the chapter is a musicological analysis of "Rosa Parks." The pertinent eschatological concepts become explosive in the interaction between the beat and the lyrical flow of Big Boi and André 3000, especially so during the breaks of the track. It is this interaction that moves the entire listening experience forward to an intimation of eschatological reality perceived as the expectation of the unexpected.

---

8. Fernando, "Aquemini."

9. Cf. Perkinson, "Underneath the MC's Wit," 14.

10. For the importance of storytelling in hip-hop, including its historical roots derived from African culture, see Cobb, *To the Break of Dawn*, 14–20. For a theology of hip-hop narratives, see Hodge, *Soul of Hip Hop*, 138–40.

11. Begbie, *Theology, Music and Time*, 5.

Part Two: Response

## THEOLOGY, TEMPORALITY, AND MUSIC

Hip-hop refuses to be approached directly by theology in any of the latter's more traditional uses. Hip-hop operates by a logic unique to its own aesthetic. This is a logic that cannot easily be sorted into typical systematic categories. Ralph Basui Watkins calls it an "Africana theology" that develops according to the unique rhythm of black culture. The concerns of such a theology, those of real-life oppression and liberation, become a "remix" of traditional systematic theology.[12] For Watkins, the theology of hip-hop is tied to a faith that is rooted in an experience initiated by God, and one that reflects on "how God has revealed himself throughout time as an agent of liberation."[13] In as much, even while giving a unique perspective on the meaning of Jesus, a theology of hip-hop enters into conversation with theology's whiter and less musical forms. It steps in through the space the cross tears in reality.

In terms of theological analysis of music's temporality, none has held more of a foundational role in recent years than the work of Jeremy Begbie. In fact, even without mention of hip-hop in particular, he concurs that music can illuminate theology to new modes of theologizing given its diverse genres. This illumination especially includes a new valuation of temporality.[14] His role here is not to set that standard for hip-hop's theology, but to offer a conversational voice against which hip-hop's own sense of time appears. The two voices meet where time ends, which has traditionally fallen under the title "eschatology." "Whatever else 'eschatology' may mean," Begbie explains, "it bespeaks a future-directedness in the Christian faith, an orientation towards a fulfillment of the purposes for which God has brought all things into being."[15] God, then, is both the basis and end of faith. The temporality of human experience begins and ends in his presence. But, time is also not monolithic. How time is perceived, what character it embodies, and what values it holds are interwoven with the particularities of lived experiences of the faithful. While Begbie's focus on the relevance of classical music for theology will emphasize certain points, offering certain readings of eschatology, hip-hop's perspective on eschatology comes from its own culture's experience of the world, in all its triumphs and struggles.

12. Watkins, *Hip-Hop Redemption*, 97.
13. Watkins, *Hip-Hop Redemption*, 97–98.
14. Begbie, *Theology, Music and Time*, 93.
15. Begbie, *Theology, Music and Time*, 98.

Perhaps surprisingly, there is a large degree of consonance between the two conversation partners, Begbie and theologies of hip-hop, on this matter. Both, in their own way, are critical of theologies that ignore temporality as it is lived, and seek to ground ultimate reality in a timeless existence somewhere beyond the world. To resist these metaphysical tendencies, both lean heavily on how God has revealed himself in time, and how this revelation is sustained by the Holy Spirit in the *Sitz im Leben* of the faithful. For Begbie, the irreplaceable revelation of the human Jesus even mandates theology to uphold some form of temporality. Through faith's assurance that Jesus is God, temporality is viewed as a gift and not a metaphysical problem to be solved.[16]

The cross is the most concentrated image in support of a theological appraisal of temporality. Beyond directing God's temporality along an eschatological trajectory, the cross reveals that God's time includes finitude. And music becomes particularly pertinent to such finitude because of its temporal nature. "Music," Begbie explains, "is constantly dying" as one note morphs into another and as one beat marks the end of its predecessor.[17] In other words, music becomes cruciform by analogous "ends."

It is along these lines that Begbie argues against theologies that hold a negative valuation of time and see the tenuous delay of God's promises as something wholly problematic. For him, delay encourages a "patience proper to Christian faith in which *something new is learned* of incalculable *value*, which cannot be learned in any other way."[18] What is learned from such lived experience, of course, will be radically different according to the form of music offered for a theological revaluation, and the culture of which the music represents. Begbie, nevertheless, makes room for such alternative, even critical, perspectives, on the basis of the variant character of music. Music is composed of difference: different orders, different notes, different rates of change, and different durations of time. It is here that enough space opens for a conversation with hip-hop's eschatology. For theologies of hip-hop, the lesson is rooted in "confronting real problems of oppression" by seeing God's self-revealing as that of the liberator. The MCs of hip-hop "relate to Jesus not as divine savior or dispenser of eternal grace, but on the level of their common understanding of what it feels like

---

16. Begbie, *Theology, Music and Time*, 97.
17. Begbie, *Theology, Music and Time*, 92.
18. Begbie, *Theology, Music and Time*, 105.

to be fucked with by those in authority."[19] More than seeing the cross as the tragedy of God's death, hip-hop perceives that this death happens from injustice. In the words of James Cone, the cross is a lynching tree.[20]

## Eschatology and Temporality

Begbie designates several eschatologically significant categories inherent to music's temporality, two of which are relevant here. To begin with, the theological dynamics of "promise and fulfillment" are correlated to music's "layered patterns of tension and resolution."[21] This category involves the idea that music, as with God's plan of redemption, takes time to develop. That it takes time for God's promise to be fulfilled does not condemn faith's desire for immediate consummation of God's grace. But Begbie's theological perspective also recognizes that this desire should be tempered by the reality of God's seemingly delayed completion. Like music, faith is called to listen to God's movement and to be patient in its happenings. When these patterns are temporally located, they create a "sense of the incompleteness of the present, that not all is given."[22] Music *hopes* in its movement and imparts such hope in those who listen to this movement.

Alongside the dynamic of promise and fulfillment is that of delay and patience. Delay, or "that things are being in some manner held back," plays a formative role in eschatology by making real that something has not yet come to pass.[23] It further shapes the hope of music. Delay is intimately linked to memory of decisive events of the past, which, in their "relative unambiguity," set what is hoped for in the future. The most obvious biblical example is the resurrection of Jesus from the dead, which is marked as the "first fruits" of the resurrection to come (1 Cor 15:20–21).

Delay is irreducibly temporal. It only occurs as what "has been" is reaching out toward what has "not yet" come. Delay straddles the divide between past and future. Begbie explicates this point by highlighting that, musically, delay "occurs especially towards the end of sections of music." This is because, on one hand, the end of the musical piece is expected by the general shape of its movement; and, on the other, its end includes a

19. Cobb, *To the Break of Dawn*, 71.
20. Cone, *Cross and the Lynching Tree*, xiii–xix.
21. Begbie, *Theology, Music and Time*, 99.
22. Begbie, *Theology, Music and Time*, 99.
23. Begbie, *Theology, Music and Time*, 99.

degree of the unexpected, which adds interest to a "predictable . . . mode of continuation."[24] Even as such, the meaning of music, in this view, comes from *resolution*. Tension serves this end primarily by refusing instant gratitude. Expectation only exists because it has been delayed, but its hope is grounded in the resolution of this delay.

The technical term for the "ends" of music is *cadence*. Begbie explains that there are two kinds of cadences: metrical, which deals with the "patterns of beats," and rhythmic, which "concerns temporal patterns of notes."[25] His exceptionally detailed section emphasizes the "perfect" or "authentic" cadence of Mozart's "Jupiter" Symphony (no. 41 in C major, 1788). In musical terms, a perfect cadence is when a movement resolves into the tonal triad of the piece—here, a C major. The resolution comes from one voice proceeding from either the seventh or fourth tone to the tonic, as another moves from the dominant to the tonic. The intricate details are less important than the overall effect, which is, as Begbie explains, to bring the music to an end in tonal *resolution*. As a point of contrast with hip-hop's ends, a common occurrence within classical cadences is that the meter either retards or dissipates completely, while the rhythmic group is augmented with additional notes to a common phrase or a surprising change in its timing. That is, tonal resolution is more significant than the temporality in which the music moves. With Begbie, "the point to emphasize is this: *cadences* are normally *metrically weak* even though they may be (and usually are) *rhythmically strong*."[26]

Even with rhythm's preeminence, music's temporality does not dissipate in classical cadences. In fact, Begbie makes the interesting point that Mozart's use of cadences effectively creates an ongoing sense of temporality. As the notes come to a resolution, they effectively begin a new measure, pushing the entire piece forward. Thus, "in one sense, the music resolves; in another it strives ahead towards resolution."[27] This interaction of ends and new beginnings is precisely what gives music its eschatological presence. Begbie even highlights that the eschatological intimation can linger even after the music has ended.

The situation in musical "ends" is precisely the opposite in hip-hop. Given that lyrical flow is relatively flat in terms of harmony, it has a

24. Begbie, *Theology, Music and Time*, 100.
25. Begbie, *Theology, Music and Time*, 125.
26. Begbie, *Theology, Music and Time*, 125.
27. Begbie, *Theology, Music and Time*, 126.

considerable lack of rhythm. But this lack has developed to emphasize the metrical complexity of a rapper's lyrics. Time takes precedence over tone in hip-hop. The genre still presents the eschatological movement that happens at its ends, as Begbie outlines. Only, its movement is eschatologically vibrant because of its metrical dissonance. Its ends are not what is expected, but what comes as unexpected.

## Flow, Cadence, and the Movement of Time

William Cobb names three constituent features of hip-hop's musical aesthetic: "'beats,' lyrics, and 'flow.'"[28] "Beat" refers to the totality of instrumentation (and not just the patterns of percussion), lyric to the words of the song, and flow to the synthesis of these two. Flow is the means by which the lyrics meld into the beat. Flow is an important aspect of what gathers the track into a single musical piece. Flow does so, on the one hand, by its inherent temporality, by being musical, and by the MC's creativity on the other. "At its heart," Cobb explains, "flow is an individual time signature, the rapper's own idiosyncratic approach to the use of time."[29] A considerable degree of the unexpectedness of hip-hop comes from its flow. This fact highlights, again, that whatever hip-hop's time brings to eschatology is rooted in the particularities of hip-hop's aesthetic.

The most comprehensive definition of flow is offered by Mitchell Ohriner, who similarly describes it as the interplay between lyrical "phrasing, rhythm, meter, rhyme, accent, patterning, and groove."[30] Ohriner goes on to distinguish between the "primary constituents" of words, phrasing, and rhythm and the "derivative constituents" of rhyme, accent, and groove. Flow happens at the "interaction between the derived constituents and meter."[31] From the perspective of listening, flow is when rhyme, accent, and groove accrue a certain meter. It is when language becomes musically temporal.

What is important here is what flow does to the track. At this more technical level, flow does much more than unite the lyrics with the beat. It augments the beat—not by doubling or following it, but by living in temporal tension with it. Flow pushes the beat forward, as it helps create the movement of the track by perpetually suggesting the meter to come. Good

28. Cobb, *To the Break of Dawn*, 14.
29. Cobb, *To the Break of Dawn*, 87.
30. Ohriner, *Flow*, 28.
31. Ohriner, *Flow*, 28.

flow rides the beat in such a way as to encourage listening. It keeps the listener engaged. It does what perfect cadence does for Mozart. But, given the rhythmic redundancy, flow does so almost entirely by its temporality. This constitutive aspect of engaged listening cannot take place if flow simply replicates the beat. Then, while flow may add a lyrical expression to the musicality of the beat, it would offer nothing in terms of temporality. The timing of flow happens through dissonance with the beat—not by wholly negating or ignoring the beat, but equally not doubling it.

At the base of flow, then, is its timing, its meter. And, by its timing, flow helps guide the expectations of the track. While these expectations can be predictable (as they often were in the early days of hip-hop), they grew to a complexity that sustains interest through unexpected turns. As Cobb continues, "Flow is the science of funking with one's own expectations of time."[32] Or, as Raekwon says after the music fades on "Rosa Parks," hip-hop tries to "enlighten" the world "with all types of flows and flavors." As Cobb's definition indicates, flow is highly individualistic. It melds with identity, as many rappers are recognized by their flow alone.[33] When it comes to the idiosyncratic characteristics of OutKast, Cobb is again helpful in describing their flow as "hyper-active, dense lines . . . wrought with double entendres and clever wordplay, all done at a speed just past the casual comprehension of the listener."[34] That OutKast's flow happens at the limit of linguistic understanding is one of the reasons why their track is suitable for such a temporal analysis.

Flow also involves cadence, which in hip-hop speaks to the division of the rhyme scheme according to the beat of the measure. Cadence indicates the breaks in lyrical content, either where one rhythmic phrase ends and another begins, or where the meter of words shifts into a new temporality. It adds an element of unexpectedness to linguistic meaning, as it flips the position of the rhyme.[35] But cadence can equally be apprehended and followed based solely on the similar phonetic aspects of the rhymes. The opening bars of both Big Boi's and André 3000's verses on "Rosa Parks" are easy illustrations of cadence (figs. 1 and 2).[36] Their flow relies heavily on a percussive

---

32. Cobb, *To the Break of Dawn*, 87–88.

33. Cf. Ohriner, *Flow*, 3.

34. Cobb, *To the Break of Dawn*, 88. This fits well if OutKast is seen as a forerunner of the crunk movement. See Cobb, *To the Break of Dawn*, 74.

35. Ohriner, *Flow*, 19–20.

36. Despite the numerous attempts to develop a transcription method for hip-hop

Part Two: Response

sixteenth-note meter, as seen in bar 19 of Big Boi's verse, and throughout André 3000's. Cadence involves when and how the meter occurs, shifts, and develops. Here, it is the interplay between the notes and rests, which complements the rhyme scheme occurring at the end of each phrase.

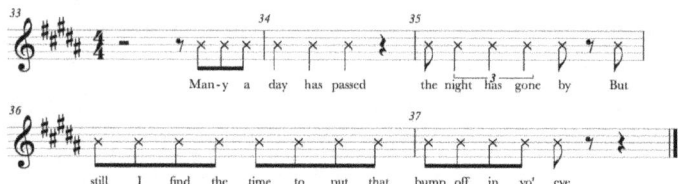

Fig. 1. OutKast, "Rosa Parks," Big Boi's verse, bars 9–11

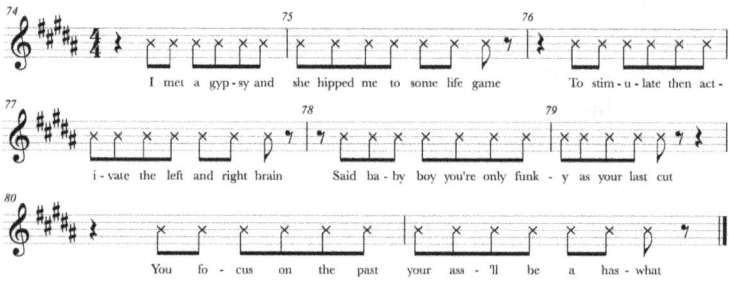

Fig. 2. OutKast, "Rosa Parks," André 3000's verse, bars 37–40

Compared with the classical definition of Begbie, cadence still refers to ends, but it is the ends of lyrical schemes and not musical phrases. Cadence for hip-hop primarily deals with meter, since tonal variation (i.e., singing) is largely absent from rap. In other terms, the ends that hip-hop's cadence indicates are metrically strong and tonally weak—the exact opposite of that from Begbie's analysis. Cadence compounds the unexpected end of flow by unpredictably shifting the lyrical meter. A simple example is in

---

analysis, I resort to the conventional Western music notation. Even the most advanced attempts, such as Mitchell Ohriner's, cannot capture the intricacies characteristic to hip-hop rhythm, such as triplet phrases, and how particular syllables align with particular notes of the underlying instruments. These transpositions are for illustrative purposes only, thereby allowing the analysis and argument to be followed even without knowledge of Western notation.

bar 39 of André 3000's verse, where the sixteenth-note rest of the previous verses is extended by an eighth note, before returning to the established pattern. In fact, the unexpected placement of cadence is a key aspect to an interesting flow.

Theologically, flow gives the beat an eschatological dimension by its idiosyncratic temporality. But this does not occur in the neatly defined "dynamic of promise and fulfilment" of which Begbie speaks. Flow pushes forward into the unexpected. It appears to hurl us toward the end by removing any comfort we may gain from a predictable knowledge of what is to come. Flow does have an end, even a resolving one. But its resolution is the lyrical punch line, the metaphor. Its end is the unexpected. Given the constitutive role of flow for hip-hop's aesthetic, however, this is precisely what is to be expected. Flow puts forth the perception of time as an expectation of the unexpected.

## TEMPORAL ANALYSIS OF "ROSA PARKS"

In "Rosa Parks" the tenuous temporalities of beat and flow represent both immediate gratification and delayed expectation, respectively. The repetition of the beat would be monotonous without the spontaneity of the flow; but, without a steady beat, the flow would itself be rhythmically chaotic. As discussed, the interaction between flow and beat is what gives hip-hop its movement and produces an aesthetic dynamic that resonates beyond the music itself into hip-hop culture and beyond. Flow is what makes hip-hop's listening experience captivating.

Part of the difficulty here is holding together the flow within a technical analysis. In some fundamental manner, analytical modes of presentation lose the fullness of aesthetic phenomena. This loss is specifically detrimental to flow, since it is a *whole* (*Gestalt*) that becomes present as more than what can be attributed to the sum of its parts. Flow is present only as the lyrics happen with the beat, as these two aspects consolidate into the track, as the flow of the track overflows into other songs, and as the artist gains a hip-hop identity associated with the particularities of their lyrical meter. All of this means, the temporal points highlighted here only gain their meaning within the track as a whole. "Rosa Parks" is unique in its particularities and would become different if any aspect was altered. Even more, given the thematic nature of *Aquemini*, the track belongs to the album, and the album finds its place in OutKast's narratival oeuvre comprising preceding

Part Two: Response

records *Southernplayalisticadillacmuzik* (1994) and *ATLiens* (1996)—all of which is outside the scope of this discussion.

## Breaks

The first temporal aspect to be analyzed, here, are the breaks in the beat that happen in measures 27, 43, and 47. Most importantly, these breaks introduce meaning by gathering attention to the track. Their musical "absence" encourages the listener to lean in, to hear the music that is happening. Not only are breaks an unexpected means of producing meaning, they occur unexpectedly in "Rosa Parks." As each happens, in their own unique ways, the entire song gains an anticipation of surprise. It is heard as a waiting for the unexpected.

The particular placing of the breaks in this track is unanticipated according to typical music standards. This goes for not only classical music but also other popular forms of music—even, to some extent, within hip-hop. It is not unusual for the beat to drop out at some point in hip-hop. Thus, there is some anticipation that it will happen. Just as, theologically, there is some anticipation that the end will come. These more predictable breaks happen at the end of the choruses (measures 16 and 36). The more unexpected breaks are shorter and more spontaneous.

The flow helps to build the unpredictability of the breaks. Throughout "Rosa Parks," the flow rides sixteenth notes. This goes for both Big Boi and André 3000. This sixteenth-note meter replicates that of the acoustic guitar, both of which are complemented by the eighth note high-hat of the drum track. There is also a rhythmic background vocal in the chorus, further encouraging the sixteenth note feel. The rhythm of the bass dances between sustained quarter and half notes and punctuated sixteenth notes.

In Big Boi's verse (fig. 3), the break in view comes after nearly two measures of straight sixteenth notes lyrical delivery, thirty-one syllables to be precise. The lyrics reach a cadence sixteenth note before the end of measure 26 and come back in after a sixteenth-note rest in measure 27. The beat, alternatively, plays through measure 26 and drops out at the start of measure 27. Simultaneously, the vocals rest for only a sixteenth note, while the beat lags behind by an additional sixteenth rest. Thus, even while replicating the sixteenth-note meter of the flow, the staggered breaks feel disjointed. They appear almost as if the producer accidentally hit the mute button on the track while the vocals were being recorded.

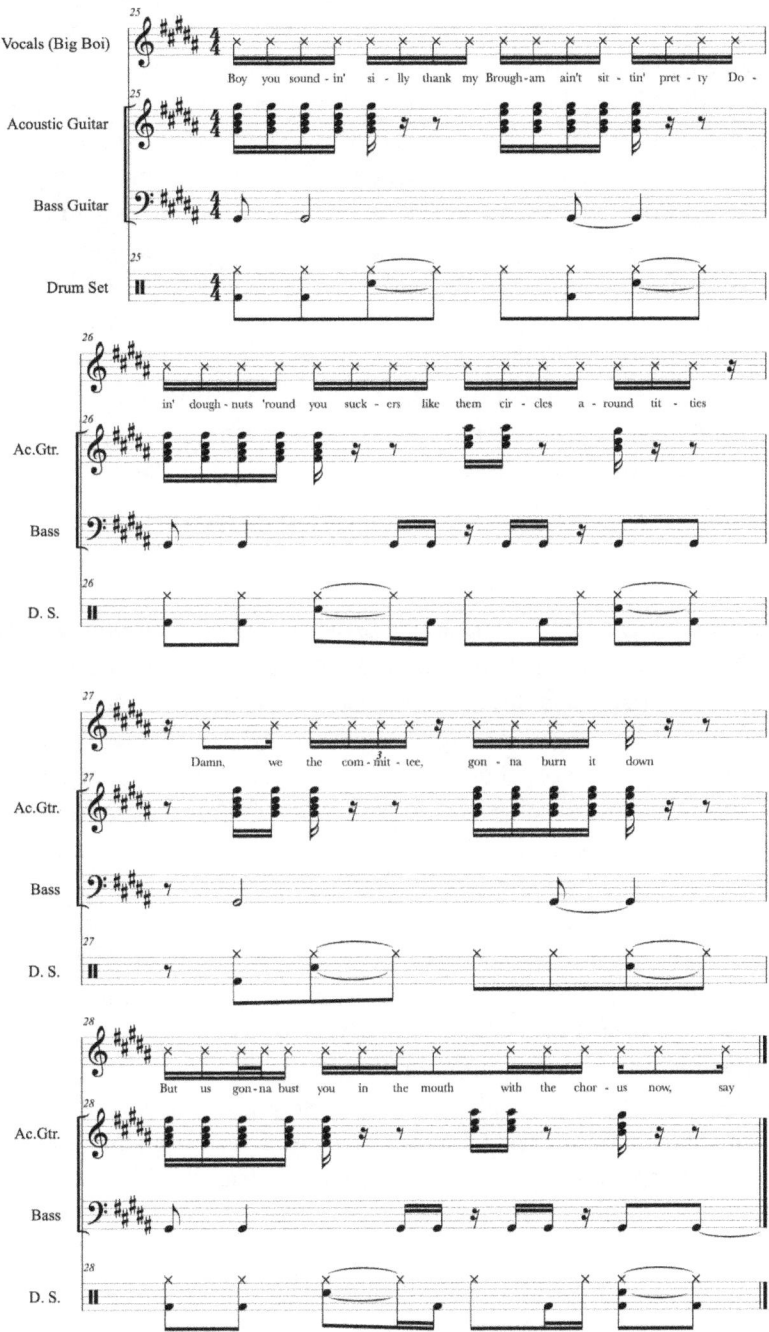

Fig. 3. OutKast, "Rosa Parks," Big Boi's verse, bars 25–28

Part Two: Response

The breaks in André 3000's verse (figs. 4 and 5) compound the unexpectation. First, the guitar drops out for the first four measures of André's verse. He flows over just the drums and bass. This variation of break foreshadows the more radical shift in the track at measure 64, when the guitar drops out again, and the bass and drums accompany a harmonica solo. Next, everything except the vocals drop out for half a measure 47 (fig. 4).

This break is at the same beat as the break in the beat of Big Boi's verse, but the flow breaks a sixteenth note into the measure. The same sort of disorientation from the break in Big Boi's verse is repeated but in a new way. Finally, in measure 47 (fig. 5), the beat drops for an entire measure. The lyrics linger into the break after another sustained run of sixteenth notes, stopping an eighth note after the bar. This break is in the same relative place as in Big Boi's verse. But, since it happens in another modification, it again appears as different than before.

## Flow

As mentioned, part of what makes the breaks in the beat unexpected is the flow. One aspect is the rapid-fire sixteenth note delivery of the lyrics; another is the subtle variations to this delivery at various places in the verses. Big Boi begins his verse as presented in fig. 1, where a relatively small number of syllables are delivered before short breaks. For the next variation, Big Boi uses a sixteenth-note triplet scheme with a rest as the middle note. This scheme gives an accent to his cadence, as heard on the lyrics: "gone-by," "your-eye"; "cha-os," "play-as"; "back-way," "bat-cave"; "geor-gia," "for-ya," and "hoy-as." Words are flexed, pushed out of their regularity, by the meter of the flow. The shift in flow gives the track a new perceptible shape, keeping the listener engaged. This development continues when these slight breaks between syllables are replaced by straight sixteenth notes leading up to the musical cadence in measure 27. The shift from the triplets to the overloaded delivery gives the track a sense of speeding up. The music is almost perceived as moving a little faster. These dynamics, then, build an anticipation that is broken in the staggered dropping out of the vocals and music.

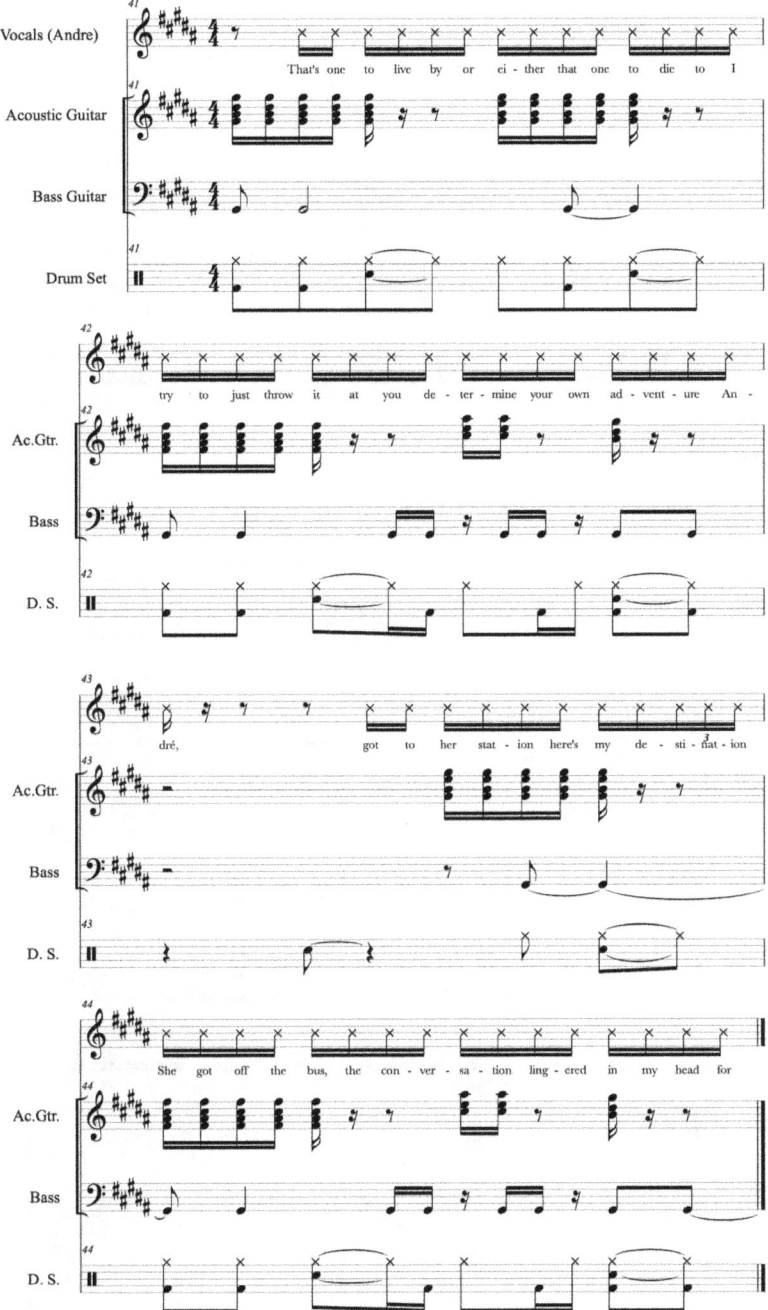

Fig. 4. OutKast, "Rosa Parks," André 3000's verse, bars 41–44

## Part Two: Response

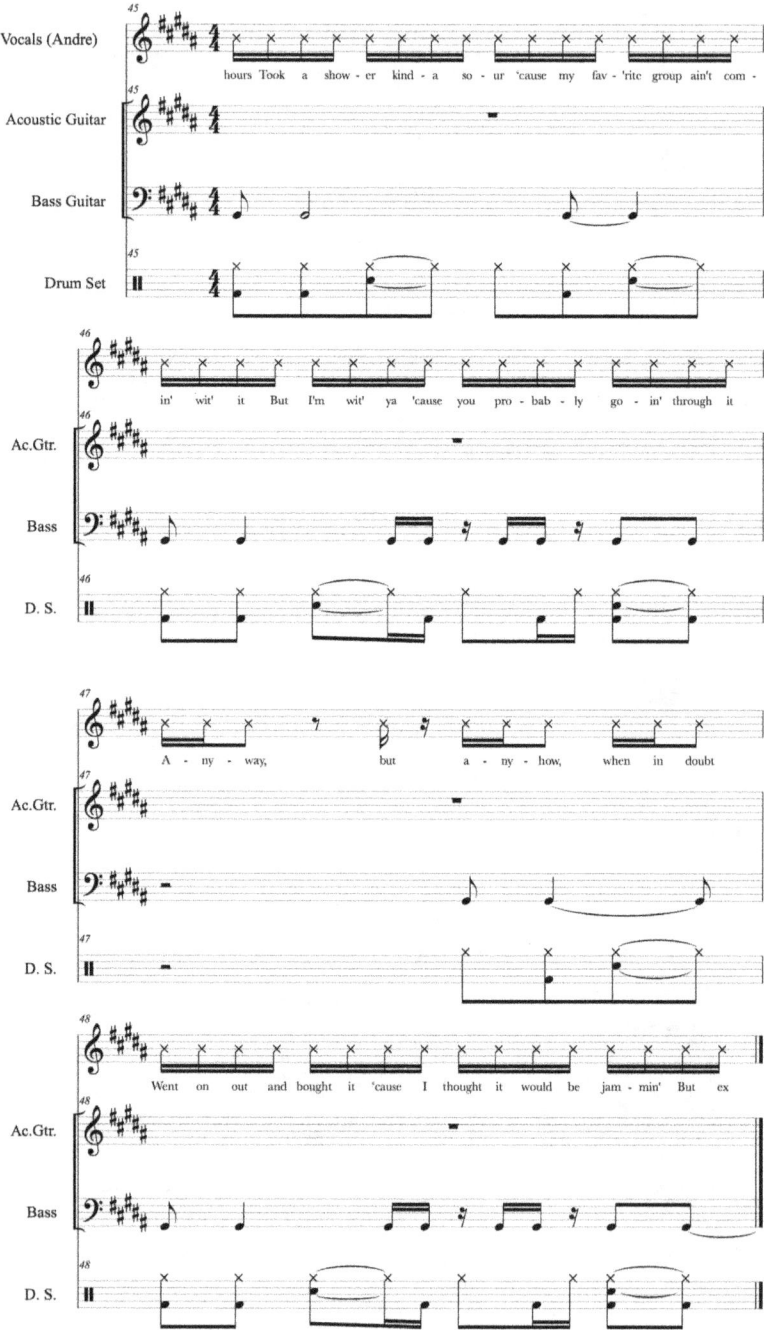

**Fig. 5.** OutKast, "Rosa Parks," André 3000's verse, bars 45–48

André 3000's verse also begins in short bursts of vocals but with a bit more consistency than Big Boi's. After four measures, his flow shifts into a succession of sixteenth notes for thirty-six beats, until the break at measure 43. From there, it picks up a flow that is somewhat reminiscent of Big Boi's triplet scheme, but here constructed with two quarter notes. He warps the words to fit this meter, and even uses neologisms to keep the flow going: "flaws-ky," "waws-ky," "aw-fully," "cost-ly," "all she." This slightly slower delivery comes as a reprieve from the fast-moving vocals of the last section. He ends the verse by speeding back up, in a flow that is similar to how it began.

The point of this temporal analysis is not to argue for some creative genius according to musical standards, but to try to convey the perception of temporality in hip-hop. Mine is an attempt to give an analysis of how the song is heard, and how it feels as it moves through its multiform variations. This analysis could be extended to include the harmonic break, which introduces the dual sense of a blues song (perhaps as a conscious effort to acknowledge hip-hop's musical roots) and a neighborhood party (which is a contextual element that could have easily inspired OutKast to include such a break). But the overall point should already be sufficiently clear: hip-hop's time moves ahead by, with, and toward the unexpected.

## TOWARD A CONCLUSION: HIP-HOP AS ESCHATOLOGY

Much happens at the ends of hip-hop's aesthetics. Hodge highlights how hip-hop culture has its own "street language" that is, among other things, formed by altering the ends of words.[37] This insight flows quite naturally into Hodge's constructive theology, as the Jesus of traditional theological expression becomes the Black Jesuz of Tupac Shakur.[38] Hip-hop's unique perspective even holds the potential to transform the meaning of death, especially united with Jesus' death on the cross.[39] More pertinent here, Hodge also highlights that a new sense of temporality is operative via this linguistic shift.

The temporality of hip-hop's wider presence follows similar trajectories to the flow's encounters with the beat in "Rosa Parks." On one hand, this temporality is rooted in the context of everyday life. It is *real* in a strong sense. It lives in the deep struggles of day-to-day life, struggles deep enough

---

37. Hodge, *Soul of Hip Hop*, 45–46.
38. Hodge, *Soul of Hip Hop*, 131–40; also Hodge, *Hip Hop's Hostile Gospel*, 166–72.
39. Hodge, *Soul of Hip Hop*, 90–101.

to shift grammatical tenses within hip-hop's language.[40] On the other hand, music has a power to "transcend you into another time and dimension."[41] One, so it seems, is held back by life; the other points to something beyond. When they combine, especially when the music of hip-hop takes the lead, they carry the transformational depth of life to the end of time. Hip-hop's temporality is a future waiting for transformation.[42]

Hodge argues that it is unhelpful for black religious traditions to adopt the eschatological stance that suffering is only temporary because the end is in sight. As he sees it, this stance says very little to "suffering is life-long, [that is] part of an ongoing social oppression."[43] Hip-hop offers a space to wrestle with questions of suffering that is detached from eschatological norms. It is a place where suffering can unite the oppressed with God. Watkins concurs, explaining that one of the failures of the church is in creating a social place closed off from the broader culture. He goes on to say that "there is much we can learn from hip-hop about how to effectively communicate—not just with the hip-hop culture but with the larger culture as well."[44] Hip-hop artists, in particular, display a peculiar ability for improvising, and for speaking the language of the common person. The point is not that hip-hop sees suffering as eternal. The point is that hip-hop doesn't bypass the reality of suffering for the sake of theological consistency. As such, hip-hop becomes relatable in a different way than traditional activities of the church. It expands the meaning of the gospel by providing a space outside of the expected. It harbors the power of transformation within its temporal flow.

James Cone powerfully explains that for the relationship of music and the black experience, "there is no attempt . . . to make philosophical distinctions between divine and human truth." Rather, "Black people accepted the dictum: Truth is experience, and experience is the Truth. If it is lived and encountered, then it is real."[45] He goes on to explain how this truth becomes expressed in the blues music from which hip-hop spurred, and that black music in the twentieth century sings of this experiential truth.

This kind of truth, born deep in the soul of struggle and resilience, is also laced within hip-hop's temporality. And, if hip-hop can serve as a

40. Hodge, *Soul of Hip Hop*, 45.
41. Hodge, *Soul of Hip Hop*, 32.
42. Dyson, "'Searching for the Black Jesus,'" 274.
43. Hodge, *Soul of Hip Hop*, 89–90.
44. Watkins, *Hip-Hop Redemption*, 134.
45. Cone, *Spirituals and the Blues*, 106.

dialogical voice with the theological formulations of the church,[46] then its eschatological flow has something theological to say. The temporality of hip-hop points forward, but not to a teleological point of simplicity.[47] Its end is a metaphor. The expectation of the unexpected of hip-hop's time is not necessarily in conflict with the expected resolution of classical sonatas and symphonies. There is an abundance in God's grace, and both dimensions are set to come. Hip-hop does highlight, however, that the resolution which God promises will come at the time and in the way that nobody knows, "except the Father" (Matt 24:36).

## BIBLIOGRAPHY

Banner, David. Foreword to *Chicken Fried Soul: Adventures in Dirty South*, edited by Tamara Palmer, 7–9. San Francisco: Backbeat, 2005.
Begbie, Jeremy. *Theology, Music and Time*. Cambridge: Cambridge University Press, 2000.
Chang, Jeff. "Introduction: Hip-Hop Arts: Our Expanding Universe." In *Total Chaos: The Art and Aesthetics of Hip-Hop*, edited by Jeff Chang, ix–xv. New York: Basic Civitas, 2006.
Cobb, William Jelani. *To the Break of Dawn: A Freestyle on the Hip-Hop Aesthetic*. New York: New York University Press, 2007.
Cone, James H. *The Cross and the Lynching Tree*. Maryknoll, NY: Orbis, 2011.
———. *The Spirituals and the Blues: An Interpretation*. New York: Seabury, 1972.
Dyson, Michael Eric. "'Searching for the Black Jesus': The Nietzschean Quest of a Metaphysical Thug." In *Open Mike: Reflections on Philosophy, Race, Sex, Culture and Religion*. New York: Basic Civitas, 2003.
Fernando, S. H., Jr. "Aquemini." *Rolling Stone*, 1998.
Hodge, Daniel White. *Hip Hop's Hostile Gospel: A Post-Soul Theological Exploration*. Leiden: Brill, 2017.
———. *The Soul of Hip Hop: Rims, Timbs and a Cultural Theory*. Downers Grove, IL: InterVarsity, 2010.
Ohriner, Mitchell. *Flow: The Rhythmic Voice in Rap Music*. Oxford: Oxford University Press, 2019.
OutKast. "Rosa Parks." Track 3 on *Aquemini*. LaFace/Arista/RCA, 1998.
Perkinson, James W. "Somewhere Underneath the MC's Wit and the Evangelical World: Toward a Christian Ethical Evaluation of Hip Hop Polemic." In *Urban God Talk: Constructing a Hip Hop Spirituality*, edited by Andre E. Johnson, 1–19. Lanham, MD: Lexington, 2013.
Rose, Tricia. *Black Noise: Rap Music and Black Culture in Contemporary America*. Hanover, NH: Wesleyan University Press, 1994.
Watkins, Ralph Basui. *Hip-Hop Redemption: Finding God in the Rhythm and the Rhyme*. Grand Rapids: Baker Academic, 2011.

---

46. Watkins, *Hip-Hop Redemption*, 99–100.
47. Hodge, *Soul of Hip Hop*, 71.

# 4

# From good kid to Wounded Healer

*Examining Kendrick Lamar's Approach to Trauma, Vocation, and Healing*

CLAUDE ATCHO

One man standin' on two words, heal everybody.
—KENDRICK LAMAR, "MOTHER I SOBER"

My life is a plot, twisted from directions that I can't see.
—KENDRICK LAMAR, "FATHER TIME"

IN 2022, KENDRICK LAMAR released his fifth album, *Mr. Morale & the Big Steppers*, a return to the musical and cultural stage which opened with a stark declaration: "I been going through something." This declaration, which Lamar tells listeners on "United in Grief," the album's first track, hints at the thematic double-helix of his much-anticipated, two-disc album: trauma and healing.

In one sense, Lamar's double-disc offering is the fulfillment of a generational hip-hop trope, a rite of passage for hip-hop legends. Hip-hop heads can with ease rattle off the double albums of icons like Wu-Tang Clan (*Wu-Tang Forever*), 2Pac Shakur (*All Eyez on Me*), Notorious B.I.G. (*Life After Death*), OutKast (*Speakerboxxx/The Love Below*), Jay-Z (*The Blueprint 2: The Gift and The Curse*), and Nas (*Street's Disciple*). The uniqueness of *Mr. Morale & the Big Steppers* emerges not from its form but its narrative content, which is indicative of Lamar's burgeoning sense of vocational responsibility, a call rooted in seeking and perpetuating healing for himself and his listeners. This vocational duty leads Lamar into territory few other mainstream hip-hop stars have traversed at the height of their artistic powers and cultural influence.[1] Lamar's offering is commendable in its aim, fascinating in its prescribed and described means and understanding of health, and worthy of theological reflection.

In this essay, I offer a brief examination of Lamar's *Mr. Morale & the Big Steppers* through a narratival and theological perspective using Henri Nouwen's paradigm of the wounded healer in order to explore Lamar's growing sense of communal responsibility and assess the vision of healing that the album advocates, particularly for black men. Lamar's sense of vocation—and the ways in which he applies this vocation in the album's narrative—suggest vital lessons on what it means to be a wounded healer, one whose wounds and wisdom can bring healing and hope to those around them.

## WHAT YOU KNOW ABOUT BLACK TRAUMA? THE PROBLEM AND THE PRESCRIPTION

Hip-hop culture's obsession with forms of toxic masculinity has been well-documented and analyzed. Such observations are not entirely invalid, though there are many artists who offer complex and contradictory alternatives—artists like Tupac Shakur who embodied both vulnerability and toxic masculinity.[2] It should also be noted these forms of toxicity, violence, oppression—what in Christian theology we rightly call sin and unrighteousness—emerge from and within systems of sin and unrighteousness.

---

1. The closest approximation is Jay-Z's *4:44*, released in 2017, which delves into his emotions, guilt, and family trauma, which contributed to his infidelity toward his wife Beyoncé. In a way, Jay-Z's honesty and vulnerability on *4:44* can be read as noteworthy while being largely precipitated by Beyoncé's public exposure of his infidelity on her 2016 album *Lemonade*. Put simply, *4:44*'s emotional transparency is reactive, not proactive.

2. Contrast, for example, Shakur's songs like "Life Goes On" or "Keep Ya Head Up" and their poignant reflections on grief and male–female relationships and songs like "Hit 'Em Up" and "All About U" and their brazen violence, threats, and misogyny.

## Part Two: Response

Hip-hop is the lingua franca, in the American context, of a people who have faced redlining, walked in the valley of the shadow of slavery and Jim Crow, navigated confinement to tenements and slums, endured abuse at the hands of unjust law enforcement, weathered poverty and have lived to place on wax a new evolution of blues and poetry that narrates, transcends, and/or participates in the trappings of their environment in the spirit of creative and defiant agency and artistry. While it is tragic yet unsurprising to see black men in particular adrift in our cities and hoods and to hear mainstream hip-hop, in many ways, amplify misogyny, nihilism, violence, and capitalistic opulence, such outcomes, though not excusable, do not exist in a vacuum; said actions and articulations live and breathe within the context of the sins of racism, classism, injustice, and trauma.

In *Healing from Racial Trauma*, Sheila Rowe proffers the following as one working definition of racial trauma: "the physical and psychological symptoms that people of color often experience after a stressful racist incident." It can be argued that black experience in America is lived within the context of racism's long shadow and persistent residue. Rowe observes the compound effect of racial trauma:

> These personal or vicarious incidents happen repeatedly, causing our racial trauma to accumulate, which contributes to a more insidious, chronic stress. When we experience a threat, our brains are wired to prepare our bodies to fight or flight. This stress response causes our nervous system, hormones, mind, and body to be on high alert. We believe we need to take immediate action against an actual threat. However, if the risk or the traumatic stress is not dealt with, our brains and bodies don't fully stand down, and we get stuck in an endless loop. Our traumatic stress triggers a physical and emotional response that then feeds our traumatic stress.[3]

Because racism is historical, personal, and systemic, the trauma faced by black Americans down the generations is staggering to comprehend, a suffering that cannot be solely grasped by the sheer recitation of facts but rather though the highest and most penetrating forms of art and vulnerability.[4]

---

3. Rowe, *Healing Racial Trauma*, 10.

4. Consider how, in particular, works of literature and autobiography have displayed with jarring poignancy that trial and trauma of black Americans, e.g., Morrison's *Beloved*, Harriet Jacobs's *The Life of a Slave Girl*, Washington's *Up from Slavery*, Wright's *Native Son*, Ellison's *Invisible Man*, and Johnson's *Middle Passage*.

From this perspective it is undeniable that for black people in America the question of healing is profoundly crucial. As a people, we carry both a triumphant and a traumatic history in our bones, bodies, and psyches. In terms of triumph and resilience, our people have made a way out of no way in large part through the power supplied by faith in God and belief in our inherent dignity—the *imago Dei*—despite society's persistent efforts to strangle the hope and life within us. In terms of trauma and suffering, whether personal, communal, or vicarious, we face social media feeds that feature the killings of black persons and watch debates on the value of black life turn into political talking points rather than a genuine pursuit of righteousness, justice, and love. The accumulation of such experience often produces a deeply felt need for healing, a way to have our wounds acknowledged, processed, and mended. Rowe highlights the dire need for reflections that guide us toward healing: "People of color have endured traumatic histories and almost daily assaults on our dignity, and we are told to get over it. We have prayed about the racism [we have experienced], been in denial or acted out in anger, but we have not known how to individually or collectively pursue healing from the racial trauma."[5] Add to this the scars and wounds that occur simply by living in a world where brokenness and pain pervade, and the need for forms of robust healing is more than apparent.

It is within the context of this admittedly brief survey of racial trauma that Lamar's vocational aims in *Mr. Morale* can be more properly situated and more fruitfully examined. Lamar presents his own summation of trauma in single biting question on "Mr. Morale": "What you know about Black trauma?" Lamar, unlike many of his rap contemporaries, seeks to not only explain what he knows of trauma but to offer a prescription to the problem of black trauma, a path to healing centered on confronting trauma as a wounded healer.

## THE JOURNEY TOWARD HEALING: READING *MR. MORALE & THE BIG STEPPERS* AS DUAL NARRATIVE[6]

To most fully analyze and appreciate the vocation of and prescription for healing offered by Lamar, I suggest a narratival reading of the album. While *DAMN.* (2017), his previous release, lent itself to speculations about

---

5. Rowe, *Healing Racial Trauma*, 15.

6. Portions of the body of this essay are derived and expanded from my short article on *Mr. Morale*. See Atcho, "Kendrick Lamar and Wounded Healers."

multiple coherent narratives, namely whether the tracklist was played in order or reverse, *Mr. Morale & the Big Steppers* operates in a straightforward narrative fashion. By tracing the broad dual narrative focus of the album and attending to the poignant and visceral movements therein, Lamar's vocation as a wounded healer and his prescription toward healing for his community emerge for consideration.

*Mr. Morale & the Big Steppers* is a masterfully crafted, brutally honest, and at times downright uncomfortable foray into the trauma, demons, and musings of one of the singular artists of this generation. And yet, the most provocative moments of the album evince a duality, focusing on Lamar's trauma and wounds while simultaneously expressing interest in the same issues experienced on a multi-layered corporate level—among black people, black men, and broader humanity. This dual narrative focus—centered on the particular and the universal, the individual and the corporate—lifts Lamar's vocation as wounded healer to the thematic foreground.

The dual narrative focus is present from the album's outset. The opening song, "United in Grief," begins with the aforementioned declaration ("I been going through something") which is then accompanied by a command: "Be afraid." Lamar's declaration and command suggest that the movement from trauma to healing is necessary and simultaneously terrifying. There is a reason many do not "do the work," as they say in common parlance, of therapy, healing, and self-reflection.[7] To resurface and reexamine personal or generational trauma is a heavy, painful endeavor, a journey which often has no set date of resolution. In *My Grandmother's Hands: Racialized Trauma and the Pathway to Mending Our Hearts and Bodies*, Resmaa Menakem describes the difference between clean and dirty pain. Clean pain "is the inescapable part of a difficult or challenging experience." However dirty pain is "avoidable," for it's the pain that emerges when one compounds their suffering and trauma through "avoidance, blame, and denial" and the refusal to process wounds.[8] Lamar has eschewed, on this album, any allegiance to dirty pain. The result is both terrible and beautiful.

The terror, it seems, emerges from the prerequisite for healing: vulnerability and truthfulness; clean pain is commendable yet deeply uncomfortable for the speaker and the audience. "Tell the truth," Lamar's fiancée,

---

7. Seattle Christian Counseling Center rightly suggests that systemic injustices against black communities have contributed to fear and resistance toward therapy. See Seattle Christian Counseling, "African Americans and the Fear of Counseling."

8. Menakem, *My Grandmother's Hands*, 76.

Whitney Alford, demands repeatedly in a chilling voice as the album opens with stark piano keys filling the soundscape. The ominous keys are accompanied by the sounds of steps—like an actor hitting the stage—as Lamar plunges into eighteen tracks of therapeutic confession. Lamar's declaration and command are in service to a quest: one man's search for healing strong enough to mend himself and cast a line of hope to all who might follow.

For Lamar, healing comes from laying everything bare and disclosing every wound: family trauma, sexual addiction, infidelity, and generational trauma. "United in Grief" offers a panoramic confession of his vices and failed coping mechanisms. "N95" bangs like a summertime bop but remains no less devoted to exposure and healing: "Take off the idols... Take off the fake deep... Take all that designer bull**** off and what do you have?" Under the mask is a wounded and warped humanity, the chorus declares in terms deeply profane. These two songs introduce the complex, individual–corporate dynamic at heart of the album. Both Lamar and this audience have been going through something. According to Lamar, we are together, as it were, bound together in a mutual garment of devastation and destiny. Lamar views his wounds and healing as necessarily bound up with the broader world around him. The "we" that constitutes his audience requires healing as urgently as he does.

Who is this corporate "we" in Lamar's view? Whether that "we" represents black folks in particular or humanity in general, the album is punctuated with the belief that Lamar's wounds are shared, microcosms of our universal wounds. The narrative of the album blends the particular and universal in order to create a moral mirror effect in which listeners find commonality in Lamar's wounds and vice versa. For instance, although it is Lamar baring his soul on the track, the title is "United in Grief," suggesting a group project, a communal share in grief and trauma. The double-helix element braids together trauma and healing thematically, and Lamar and his audience narratively.

Similar in effect is "We Cry Together," a brutal, lewd, vulgar duet that gives new meaning to the notion of a hard listen. Built on vicious barbs tossed back and forth between Lamar and actress Taylour Paige, the song can be interpreted at a distance, as a reflection of Lamar and his fiancée's relational strife introduced in the album's opening song. Yet, the song is prefaced with an indictment upon all: "This is what the world sounds like." Lamar wants listeners to reckon with the toxicity we experience as listeners, not as simply as his mess but ours too. Thus, the album's narrative through line exists on two planes of meaning—the particulars of Lamar's wounds and the universality of our wounds as black people and humanity as a whole—often weaving, overlapping, and intersecting.

This communal or universal narrative can also be found on "Worldwide Steppers" through both its title and its narrative themes. Though the song details, in coarse terms, Lamar's personal sexual addiction, the title implicates others, as does the final verse ("Eight billion people on Earth, silent murderers)" and the hook ("We some killers, walkin' zombies, tryna scratch that itch"). All of this amounts to Lamar's own particular spin on Rom 3:23, "all have fallen short of the glory of God . . . ." According to Lamar's moral vantage point, all are wounded, implicated, and fall short of being whole and healed. Whether we admit it or not, we are united in grief and toxicity—and the need for healing.

The album's dual narrative focus—Lamar's grief and trauma and that of the corporate "we"—reshapes how listeners engage the album. This dual focus strips away the ability to listen voyeuristically and prompts, in place of such musical tourism, a call to engaged reflection. Indeed, to listen to *Mr. Morale & the Big Steppers* and only attend to Lamar's quest for peace and healing, but not one's own, is to miss the deep, dual narrative structure of the album.

The album's entire whole is concerned with both the personal and corporate. It seems that the "big steppers" to which the album title refers are those in a long and universal line marching to the drumbeat of "calamities on repeat" ("Savior") and unwilling to unmask their wounds and grief, numbing and hiding behind consumerism ("N95"). Then the persona Mr. Morale—on disc two—enters to offer a path toward healing by virtue of a "breakthrough" according to the first song on disc two, "Count Me Out." Then, and only then, through this breakthrough can we step together into wholeness.

## HENRI NOUWEN, KENDRICK LAMAR, AND THE VOCATION OF A WOUNDED HEALER

This dual narrative dynamic illumines one of the more fascinating aspects of *Mr. Morale & the Big Steppers*, Lamar's vocational direction and quest as Mr. Morale. Here Lamar leverages and stewards his trauma for a communal purpose. He announces his intent on "Mother I Sober," declaring, "One man standin' on two words, heal everybody." Lamar's performance and vulnerability sync up to form a vocational approximation of a wounded healer.

## From good kid to Wounded Healer—ATCHO

In *The Wounded Healer: Ministry in Contemporary Society*, Henri Nouwen, Catholic priest and writer, describes a wounded healer as one who "make[s] their own wounds available as a source of healing."[9] While Nouwen's work is particularly suited toward those who serve in Christian ministry, his insights and observations reach well beyond the clerical. Nouwen presciently analyzed loneliness and isolation as critical wounds present at each tier of personal and social experience, describing the conditions of the suffering world, a suffering generation, a suffering person, and a suffering minister.[10] Nouwen likens each mode of suffering to "four doors" through which a minister, if they are to follow Christ and serve the world, must enter to be of faithful service in the wounded world. According to Nouwen, the minister or leader can only be transformative in their impact through a deep awareness of wounds—both theirs and those whom they serve. Nouwen contends in no uncertain terms: "For the minister is called to recognize the sufferings of his time in his own heart and make that recognition the starting point of his service. Whether he tries to enter into a dislocated world, relate to a convulsive generation, or speak to a dying man, his service will not be perceived as authentic unless it comes from a heart wounded by the suffering about which he speaks."[11] Nouwen acknowledges that the notion of a wounded healer may seem counterintuitive at best and neurotic at worst. He notes that for some the concept may seem "morbid and unhealthy," a concept in which "pain is romanticized instead of criticized." Nouwen's belief in wounds as a source of healing in and through a leader rests upon his understanding of hospitality. Before one can truly welcome another, one must be at home in themselves, aware of their wounds and isolations, through which they can truly attend to the wounds of another. Nouwen explains hospitality as "the virtue which allows us to break through the narrowness of our own fears and to open our houses to the stranger."[12] Thus for Nouwen the question "What does hospitality as a healing power require?" is accompanied with the simple yet hard-won answer: "It requires first of all that the host feel at home in his own house, and secondly that he create a free and fearless place for the unexpected visitor."[13]

9. Nouwen, *Wounded Healer*, 2.

10. Though it is beyond the scope of this short essay to attend to Nouwen's diagnosis for each category of suffering, in brief, he traces the root of the malady to historical fragmentation, loss of meaning, isolation, loss of loving authority, and familial abandonment.

11. Nouwen, *Wounded Healer*, 1.

12. Nouwen, *Wounded Healer*, 88.

13. Nouwen, *Wounded Healer*, 89.

## Part Two: Response

Hospitality, in Nouwen's framework, is flanked by two key supporting conceptions: "concentration and community." Concentration is the strength of character and prayerful reflection that enables the minister or leader to comprehend their internal world and experiential wounds in a mature manner. For concentration also carries a protective function: it "prevents the minister from burdening others with his pain and allows him to accept his wounds as helpful teachers of his own and his neighbor's condition."[14] Community is the mature sharing of wounds in mutual recognition and Godward hope. Nouwen writes, "Community arises where the sharing of pain takes place, not as a stifling form of self-complaint, but as a recognition of God's saving promises."[15] Hospitality, enacted through concentration and community, produce the "recognition" that our wounds are not the final word, but through the company of wounded healers, such recognition and vulnerability encourage us to endure and to look toward the God of hope and healing.

At this point, some of the essential ways in which Lamar functions in the approximate mode of Nouwen's wounded healer come into clearer view. First, Lamar opts to embrace rather than refuse the vocational task of the wounded healer. The words from "Mother I Sober"—"One man standin' on two words, heal everybody"—stand as an ordination of sorts, a plunge into the vocation of a wounded healer wielding a mic to broadcast his wounds to millions. We must be careful to not overlook the commendation Lamar deserves for taking up such a task. Many modern notable hip-hop stars have faced traumas and adverse childhood experiences similar to what Lamar outlines—experiences classified as Adverse Childhood Experiences ("ACEs"). ACEs are defined as "potentially traumatic events that occur in childhood, ranging from abuse and neglect to other traumatic experiences derived from household dysfunction."[16] Prominent hip-hop stars like Lil Wayne, Jay-Z, Tupac, and Meek Mill have broadcast their complex experience of trauma, racism, and "ACEs" to millions of listeners around the global, but rarely do their sustained musical offerings proscribe a way toward healing and change.[17] Family and trauma therapist Kenneth V. Hardy

---

14. Nouwen, *Wounded Healer*, 94.
15. Nouwen, *Wounded Healer*, 94.
16. Cummings and Conrad, "'Mind Playing Tricks on Me.'"
17. See Meek Mill, "Trauma"; Jay-Z, "You Must Love Me"; and 2Pac Shakur's "Trapped," "Changes," "Brenda's Got a Baby." Justin Tinsley details Lil Wayne's traumatic past, reading his 2018 album, *Tha Carter V*, as a "triumph over trauma," though Wayne offers little in the way of guiding listeners toward healing in the manner of Lamar.

writes that "racial oppression is a traumatic form of interpersonal violence which can lacerate the spirit, scar the soul, and puncture the psyche."[18] These artists have given voice in their varied ways to their scars, but it is Lamar who offers something more prescient and prescriptive. He offers his wounds in an effort to "heal everybody."

Secondly, Lamar offers a step toward healing by the examination and articulation of his internal and experiential pain, probing his wounds honestly rather than denying them in the name of an invulnerable masculinity. Forms of masculinity that demand men show no emotion, weakness, or tears are often a coping mechanism, a way to endure against an incessant deluge of pain, trauma, and indignities. Lamar speaks to such realities on "Father Time" ("'Cause if I cried about it, he'd surely tell me not to be weak / Daddy issues, hid my emotions, never expressed myself . . . Man should never show feelings, being sensitive never helped"). Lamar charts a new path of open-hearted masculinity, a breath of fresh air for hip-hop as a genre as it hits its fiftieth birthday. Lamar's vulnerability, and the articulation thereof, is integral to the task of a wounded healer. Nouwen observes that the wounded leader faces the massive and "dramatic" task: they "must come to terms with the inner tremendum."[19] They must become "the articulator of inner events."[20] This point is critical to Nouwen's project and I believe vital to grasping the import of Lamar's vocational task. It merits attending to Nouwen in full:

> The key word here is articulation. The man who can articulate the movements of his inner life, who can give names to his varied experiences, need no longer be a victim of himself, but is able slowly and consistently to remove the obstacles that prevent the spirit from entering. He is able to create space for Him whose heart is greater than his, whose eyes see more than his, and whose hands can heal more than his. This articulation, I believe, is the basis for a spiritual leadership of the future, because only he who is able to articulate his own experience can offer himself to others as a source of clarification.[21]

---

Tinsley, "Lil' Wayne's 'Carter V' Is a Triumph over Trauma."
18. Hardy, "Healing the Hidden Wounds of Racial Trauma."
19. Nouwen, *Wounded Healer*, 38.
20. Nouwen, *Wounded Healer*, 38.
21. Nouwen, *Wounded Healer*, 38.

## Part Two: Response

Nouwen dubs the one who can articulate the movements of their inner life—pain, longings, wounds, and all—as "tomorrow's leader," the one who can usher an inward generation toward awareness, openness, community, and hope. Leveraged as a frame for the album, Lamar excels in articulation, even if that articulation consists of traumas, coping mechanism, and toxicity listeners would prefer not to countenance or hear. On "N95," Lamar articulates the false coping mechanisms of consumerism, materialism, and mammon. On "Worldwide Steppers," Lamar indicts himself for turning to sex as a numbing device for deeper wounds. Such articulations are indeed a clarification to listeners who in the album's dual narrative are to recognize their journey toward healing as intertwined with Lamar's. We are united in grief and woundedness and, possibly, in healing as well.

In the wake of the #MeToo movement, Lamar's articulation takes a particularly transparent form in his discussion of sexual abuse, which offers a path to openness and healing in particular for men who have suffered abuse. On "Mother I Sober," Lamar details the trauma he suffered when his family believed Lamar was abused sexually by his cousin. Lamar raps that he denied this ever happened, but his parents refusal to believe him became a form of "gaslighting" in reverse: he began to think the abuse did happen. Lamar reveals on the song that his mother herself was sexually abused, and this trauma shaped how she responded to him. Lamar dubs this generational trauma, and notes that many black men have suffered similarly. He raps:

> I know the secrets, every other rapper sexually abused
> I see 'em daily burying the pain in chains and tattoos
> So listen close before you start to pass judgement on how we move . . .
> This is post-traumatic Black families . . .

Lamar's articulation opens the pathway for listeners—particularly black men—to find in his wounds a place to examine their own. Indeed, a tide is turning in hip-hop, in which rappers have spoken of their experiences of abuse.[22] Though it would be hasty to conflate correlation with causation, it is equally naive to deny the influence of Lamar's vulnerability. Potentially, more relevant for this essay is Lamar's reading of his vulnerability—he sees it as breaking generational curses. The female voice which entered on the album's first song returns on "Mother I Sober" to narrate our interpretation of Lamar's articulation of wounds and trauma, stating,

---

22. The most recent example is revered rapper Phonte Coleman, of Little Brother, on Black Milk's "No Wish" (2023) as well as the Little Brother documentary *May the Lord Watch*.

"You did it, I'm proud of you / You broke a generational curse." The song ends with a pseudo choral voice declaring, "I bare my soul and now we're free." Note again the dual focus of the particular ("*I* bare my soul") and the corporate ("*we're* free"). Here is the liberative impact and causation of the wounds opened by the healer.

Finally, Lamar's attention to personal and communal wounds aligns with the genuine task of the wounded healer. Nouwen writes, "Making one's own wounds a source of healing, therefore, does not call for a sharing of superficial personal pains but for a constant willingness to see one's own pain and suffering as rising from the depth of the human condition which all men share."[23] Recall "Worldwide Steppers" and its totalizing claim on our shared immortality, and the album's narrative insistence that listeners engage the album personally, stripping away the ability to listen voyeuristically without reflection. Lamar's wounds are interconnected with all wounds.

## COMPLICATIONS OF A WOUNDED HEALER

Like any critical analysis, there are limits and weakness to the wounded healer reading that I offer. Perhaps more a notable complication of my analysis is that Lamar explicitly refuses any messianic mantle or concomitant heroic adulation for his articulation and vulnerability. Though Lamar positions himself as a wounded healer through the album, especially on disc two, on "Savior" he also rejects all man-made messiahs: "Kendrick made you think about it, but he is not your savior / [J.] Cole made you feel empowered, but he is not your savior." Lamar may be of two minds here. For how does this messianic repudiation fit his salvific mantra: "One man standin' on two words, heal everybody"? For Lamar, it seems the distinction is his own flawed humanity. "The cat is out the bag," he rhymes, "I am not your Savior / I find it just as difficult to love thy neighbors." Lamar is akin to a wounded healer, not on the basis of a greater morality, but on the basis of a greater vulnerability—the articulation which Nouwen attributes to tomorrow's leaders. The proverbial cat was in the bag when audiences viewed Lamar as morally upright and heroic—without significant wounds. But the truth is now out by Lamar's own articulation. Critic Charles Holmes puts it well: "Kendrick's fifth studio album is about what happens when a rapper hailed as 'the voice of a generation' removes the metaphorical mask . . . and reveals that what's underneath is far uglier, more broken, and more

23. Nouwen, *Wounded Healer*, 88.

## Part Two: Response

forthright than most had imagined."[24] It is this truth of woundedness that carries possibilities of healing that Lamar's assumed heroism could truly reach. It seems then Lamar offers implicitly the hope that we too can be wounded healers by sharing our vulnerability rather than pretending to possess a flawless past or a perfect morality.

As with any worthwhile artistic offerings, complications do abound. Vulnerability, though commendable, is not enough for deep healing—in life or even in the album's narrative. Articulation, vulnerability, and hospitality combine to construct a *step* into healing, a much-needed one, but a step is far from reaching the metaphorical finish line. Throughout the album, Lamar's vulnerability is framed, guided, and interpreted by sampled audio from Eckhart Tolle, a teacher on spiritual enlightenment who borrows from Zen Buddhism, Sufism, Hinduism, and the Bible. Tolle is, in effect, the album's spiritual director, the Virgil to Lamar's Dante, guiding him through terrifying emotional terrain toward the paradise of healing. On disc one's "Father Time," Eckhart is subtly introduced by the album's recurring female voice. The song begins with the female voice stating to Lamar, "You really need some therapy," who offers the standard invulnerable masculinity known in hip-hop, "Real nigga need no therapy, f*ck you talkin' about?" The woman replies, "Reach out to Eckhart."

The clearest instance of Tolle's subtle centrality is "Mr. Morale," the culmination of the album's journey and the moment of transformation. The song begins with the heavy breathing of a detoxing man and the guttural groans of a body experiencing the shedding of skin—in this case the shedding of trauma—to emerge new and whole. Tolle offers the final word, suggesting that such insights, paired with deep vulnerability, form the basis of transcendent freedom from generational traumas. For this the reason "Mr. Morale" is followed by "Mother I Sober." Lamar has detoxed from societal masks and false coping mechanisms of grieving in order to confront his pain clear-eyed and to assess the complex generational ways trauma has bound and warped him and us, his family, and black culture at large. Now, he assumes more fully the posture of a wounded healer.

While Lamar declares explicitly that "he is not your savior," the album leaves open the door of possibility that Tolle's insights just might be. The message seems to be that good, thorough therapy is what it takes to heal from personal and generational wounds. Tolle's inclusion suggests a discernible shift in Lamar's portrayal of religion through his albums, from the

---

24. Holmes, "To Pimp a Therapist."

Christian motifs of *good kid, m.A.A.d city*, the exploration of Hebrew Israelite perspectives on *DAMN.*, and now the enlightened spirituality of Mr. Morale. On his 2012 album, *good kid, m.A.A.d city*, the album's narrative spiritual climax features Lamar, guided by a neighborhood woman, praying the sinner's prayer, a common plea of faith and repentance.[25] Contrasted with *Mr. Morale & the Big Steppers*, Lamar's musical persona, under Tolle's guidance, has evolved from that simple faith to something seemingly more complex and syncretic while taking up the aforementioned vocational task. Lamar comments on this evolution on "Mother I Sober": "Where's my faith? / Told you I was Christian, but just not today / I transformed, prayin' to the trees, God is taking shape." In moving toward healing, it seems, Lamar has moved tentatively toward new spiritual ground.

Potentially, the most problematic aspect of the healing described and proscribed by Lamar, guided by Tolle, is the lack of systematic awareness. Tolle's guidance and Lamar's declaration suggest an over-realizing healing, as if the Lamar of the album will now exist in a world where traumas no longer exist, persons no longer fall prey to vices, systems no longer oppress, abuse no longer occurs, and racism and sin no longer assault. Thus, there are two notable theological issues present in Lamar's Tolle-guided healing. These issues do not counter what is commendable in Lamar's exploration but serve as critical complications worthy of note.

First is the recognition of the shortcomings of Lamar's syncretistic Tolle-guided path for Christian believers. Rather than speculate on another's faith, listeners might ponder how Lamar's journey might help us better understand our own. His bold affirmation that he is wounded and his bold refusal of the role of savior remind us that at the heart of the Christian faith stands one who is truly both, which we will explore in brief shortly.

Second is the recognition that it is within Christian teaching that one finds resources for the therapeutic and systematic analyses and solutions. The album offers the suggestion that good therapy heals generational traumas without reckoning with the fact that healed people still exist in a traumatic, brutal world.[26] Christian teaching, specifically the teaching of Jesus—the consummate wounded healer—offers both balm for personal wounds and a vision for a new societal relation. This gap within the album's

---

25. *good kid, m.A.A.d city* opens with the sinner's prayer on the introductory song, "Sherane a.k.a Master Splinter's Daughter," and on "Sing About Me, I'm Dying Of Thirst."

26. In *Trauma and Race*, Sheldon George argues that in conversing categories of race, we converse trauma. Thus in the terms we have been using in this essay, true healing would requiring the undoing of racialized identities.

narrative and scope by contrast shows the resources latent within the large house that is Christian teaching and tradition to address both the personal and systematic.

## IMPLICATIONS OF READING *MISTER MORALE & THE BIG STEPPERS* THROUGH THE WOUNDED HEALER LENS

The Christian gospel declares that it is Jesus of Nazareth who is the world's true wounded healer, pierced for our transgressions and by whose wounds we are healed (Isa 53:5). The early church applies Israel's servant songs in Isaiah to Jesus to such an extent that Isaiah was deemed the fifth gospel. Down the centuries, the church has believed Christ to be our wounded healer. By his traumatic wounds, he mends our own. The crucifixion of Jesus finds its closest modern horrific parallel in the black pain of lynching as theologian James Cone has written of powerfully in his groundbreaking work *The Cross and the Lynching Tree*.[27] That God incarnate would descend to such suffering proves a deep divine solidarity with all who suffer in this world. There is then—if applied properly—great hope and healing power in the Christian gospel for wounds and trauma, particularly those of the black community which Lamar describes. It is worth noting that Christ is also the world's wounded healer, for it is his wound—the vulnerable sacrifice of his broken body—that gives life to the whole world. This notion of healing—and Christ as the wounded healer—is often lost when salvation is considered only as a forensic exchange, in which Christ's wounds pay for sin's penalty, but the reality of Christ's wounds as a balm of healing for our experiential wounds sits silently in the background.

In this sense, Lamar's winding journey is a helpful corrective for audiences of faith. Within the reading I offer, Lamar's project illustrates why individual believers and faith communities must take up the urgent ministry of the wounded healer through the work of introspection, articulation, and hospitality to offer spaces in which wounds can be processed in the light of faithful community around the world's wounded healer, Christ.[28] Such

---

27. I engage further with Cone and the various "images" of the atonement as applied to black experience in the chapter "Jesus" in *Reading Black Books*.

28. Creative ways in which black Christians are finding ways to move toward wholeness and healing can be seen in offerings on prayer by authors like Cole Arthur Riley. For ways in which communal healing can occur through memory and communal spaces, see

practices and spaces are rare among men—black men in particular—and are deeply needed.

Lamar is boldly transparent about his pain, wounds, and sins. Where are ordinary men—the masses who make up his fandom—offered the same spaces and avenues for safe transparency? Where do such spaces exist for women? What is needed is distinct from the generic proliferation of "therapy-speak," in which therapeutic terms spread exponentially into common conversations and our cultural lexicon and are used haphazardly. Equally problematic is that the uninformed proliferation of therapy-speak often leads to people posturing as "the language of suffering often finds its way into the mouths of those who suffer least."[29] Contra such errors, there is great need for an upswell of communities that will take seriously the experiences of trauma, personal and generational, *and* the hope of the Christian gospel, applied to this life and the life to come, all of which emerges from the suffering, sympathy, and victory of the true wounded healer, Christ. A wounded healer reading of Lamar's 2022 album suggests these questions be taken up urgently in theory and in practice, lest in pointing out some of the trappings of Lamar's description toward healing, we fall prey to the trap of offering no tangible solutions of our own.

## BIBLIOGRAPHY

Atcho, Claude. "Kendrick Lamar and Wounded Healers." *Think Christian*, May 31, 2022. https://thinkchristian.net/kendrick-lamar-and-wounded-healers.
———. *Reading Black Books: How African American Literature Can Make Our Faith More Whole and Just*. Grand Rapids: Brazos, 2022.
Cone, James H. *The Cross and the Lynching Tree*. Maryknoll, NY: Orbis, 2011.
Cummings, André Douglas Pond, and Caleb Gregory Conrad. "From 'Mind Playing Tricks on Me' to 'Trauma': Adverse Childhood Experiences and Hip Hop's Prescription." *Washburn Law Journal* 59 (2020) 267–300. https://lawrepository.ualr.edu/faculty_scholarship/257/.
George, Sheldon. *Trauma and Race: A Lacanian Study of African American Racial Identity*. Waco, TX: Baylor University Press, 2016.
Hardy, Kenneth V. *The Enduring, Invisible, and Ubiquitous Centrality of Whiteness*. New York: Routledge, 2015.
———. "Healing the Hidden Wounds of Racial Trauma." *Reclaiming Children and Youth* 22 (Spring 2013) 24–28.

---

my reading of Toni Morrison's *Beloved* in *Reading Black Books*.

29. Waldman, "Rise of Therapy-Speak."

## Part Two: Response

Holmes, Charles. "To Pimp a Therapist: Kendrick Lamar's Messy, Complicated 'Mr. Morale & the Big Steppers.'" *The Ringer*, May 16, 2022. https://www.theringer.com/2022/05/16/music/kendrick-lamar-mr-morale-big-steppers-review.

Lamar, Kendrick. *Mr. Morale & the Big Steppers*. Top Dawg Entertainment/Aftermath/Interscope, 2022. Digital album.

Menakem, Resmaa. *My Grandmother's Hands: Racialized Trauma and the Pathway to Mending Our Hearts and Bodies*. Las Vegas: Central Recovery, 2017.

Nouwen, Henri J. M. *The Wounded Healer: Ministry in Contemporary Society*. New York: Image, 1979.

Rowe, Sheila Wise. *Healing Racial Trauma: The Road to Resilience*. Downers Grove, IL: InterVarsity, 2020.

Seattle Christian Counseling. "African Americans and the Fear of Counseling: A Christian Counselor's Thoughts." Sept. 21, 2013. https://seattlechristiancounseling.com/articles/african-americans-and-the-fear-of-counseling-a-christian-counselors-thoughts.

Tinsley, Justin. "Lil Wayne's 'Carter V' Is Triumph over Trauma." Andscape, Oct. 11, 2018. https://andscape.com/features/lil-wayne-carter-v-is-triumph-over-trauma-abuse-suicide-attempt-jail-time-lawsuits-natural-disaster/.

Tolle, Eckhart. *The Power of Now: A Guide to Spiritual Enlightenment*. Novato, CA: New World Library, 1999.

Waldman, Katy. "The Rise of Therapy-Speak: How a Language Got off the Couch and into the World." *New Yorker*, Mar. 26, 2021. https://www.newyorker.com/culture/cultural-comment/the-rise-of-therapy-speak.

# 5

# Back on Beat

*A Theology of Socioeconomics and Solidarity in Akrobatik's "Remind My Soul"*

Krystal Berry

"Yeah, it's gettin' wild out here . . ."[1] is the opening phrase of the song "Remind My Soul," written by hip-hop artist Akrobatik, and the phrase seems to echo beyond its 2003 debut. Perhaps the current reality is that it's *been* wild out here! In a wild time of global warming that causes unprecedented natural disasters around the world but where industrialism remains priority, a wild time where cyber ethics seem to be lost in the sea of anti-intellectualism and dishonesty, a wild time of antithetical Christian Nationalism idolized by those who dare speak the name of the One who fought against the very things they stand for, or a wild time of "wars and rumors of wars" where countries indeed have the right to defend themselves but go on to commence and sustain the genocide of a people long-oppressed by them: it's *been* wild out here.

These are just a few facets of the "wild" times experienced by Americans, yet there is another lens into the black American experience today. It is a wild time of economic instability—especially for blacks in America. It

1. Akrobatik, "Remind My Soul."

## Part Two: Response

is a wild time of race-based trauma that has always existed and taken a toll on the mental health of blacks in America. It is a wild time of healthcare disparities where there are pleas for Americans who work in healthcare to "Listen to the Whispers Before the Screams"[2] as advocates continue to highlight the crisis of black maternal healthcare in America. It is a wild time of incarcerated black Americans in state prisons "at nearly five times the rate of white Americans."[3] It is a wild time of poverty in the black community where hustle culture is praised in an effort to make a decent living but could be a response to the fear of poverty that has haunted black people for centuries in America. Though not exhaustive, much of this speaks to the socioeconomic issues that have long burdened black America.

Akrobatik writes these lyrics with a centuries-old history of blacks in America, and the early 2000s saw some of these same issues. "Remind My Soul" is the ingenious work of the hip-hop artist Akrobatik, otherwise known as Jared Bridgeman. "He is an American rapper from the Dorchester neighborhood of Boston, Massachusetts. He is also a part of the hip-hop duo The Perceptionists with Mr. Lif."[4] An associate lecturer at the University of Massachusetts-Boston and a native of Boston, Akrobatik fully understands the plight of blacks in his community. His music has been inundated with the truths of his experiences, as well as the experiences of others like him.

"In contrast to the presumptions of postwar liberalism, activists involved with the early Civil Rights movement believed that segregation and discrimination were not simply Southern problems but were prevalent throughout the nation."[5] Like those committed to the equality and equity of Blacks in America, "hidden figures" who chose to contribute to the civil rights movement did so in their respective communities even if those efforts would not be as well known. Akrobatik is among those Hip-hop artists who choose to use their voices to address injustices that affect the black community, bringing awareness to a city and/or situation that may not have been the focal point of civil rights movements but certainly had a movement of their own—reiterating the words of Dr. Martin Luther King Jr., who reminds us, "Injustice anywhere is a threat to justice everywhere. We

---

2. Njoku et al., "Listen to the Whispers Before They Become Screams," 438.

3. Nellis, "Color of Justice."

4. Jared Bridgeman, LinkedIn profile, accessed May 16, 2023, https://www.linkedin.com/in/akrobatikmc/.

5. Horton, *Race and the Making of American Liberalism*, 140.

are caught in an inescapable network of mutuality, tied in a single garment of destiny. Whatever affects one directly, affects all indirectly."[6]

Briefly, "Remind My Soul" alludes to the external issues that overwhelmed and continue to overwhelm the black community within Boston. Primarily, the song examines what he sees as internal issues between blacks that include the presence of self-hate and a selfish nature that seems to promote an "every-man-for-himself" reality. Through his music, Akrobatik not only speaks to the issues of his community, but he simultaneously reminds his listeners of the work and witness of those activists and leaders mentioned in his music, including but not limited to Harriet Tubman, Malcolm X, Bob Marley, Nat Turner, Arthur Ashe, and Dr. Martin Luther King Jr. While the song does name the issues of the black experience in Boston, it simultaneously contains a repetitive hope that the state of the black (wo)man can be improved as he repeats the phrase, "Remind my soul."

The concerns raised by Akrobatik are holy concerns, and they are likewise ever present. This essay is not an attempt to bring resolution to the work of Akrobatik specifically, because this work is still in progress. Isabel Wilkerson names the ongoing work of addressing injustice when she likens the work of justice to an old house in her book *Caste: The Origins of Our Discontent*. "With an old house, the work is never done, and you don't expect it to be. America is an old house. We can never declare the work over."[7] With this in mind, while this essay will highlight the prophetic witness of "Remind My Soul" and the value of the voice of hip-hop in its quest to continue dismantling the old house of socioeconomic oppression, it will also highlight Akrobatik's introspective look into the black community to suggest how this work must also be addressed from within. Further into this essay, it will be helpful to look at the internal factors that create the self-inflicted wounds of which Akrobatik speaks. Initially, it will be important to examine the external factors that aid in the oppression of black people. Through raising awareness concerning poverty, discrimination, health disparities, and even economic equality within the black community, "Remind My Soul," like other songs of hip-hop, speaks to the consciousness of America and the black community as it reminds our souls of the past, rededicates them to the present, and encourages the black community to remain resilient for the future.

---

6. King, "Letter from Birmingham Jail."
7. Wilkerson, *Caste*, 15.

Part Two: Response

## TACKLING THE EXTERNAL OPPOSITION ("OPPS")

The "wild" state of humanity of which Akrobatik speaks reflects the external issues of the black community that did not exist simply in Boston but also throughout the domestic United States and the world. It is important to frame the external issues that already exist before looking into the internal struggles of the black community named in Akrobatik's lyrics. Blacks were and are already up against an abundance of social injustices that pervaded and continue to pervade American culture. Specifically in Boston, these include injustices related to discriminatory busing practices, housing inequities, poverty, and discrepancies in crime reporting to name a few. For centuries up till present-day, particularly in America,

> Every social system is made up of separate but interlinked and interdependent institutions, both public and private, that are designed to meet one or more needs of the public; the most important include education, business enterprises and employment, government at all levels, healthcare, the legal system (including policing, courts, and imprisonment), and even religion. Each of these institutions, from their inception in colonial times was established, maintained and perpetuated by White men, who have never constituted a majority of the American population.[8]

In a society where colonizers desire and aspire to lord over others, those who support caste systems (or systems that are maintained by social hierarchy) must set up social and economic systems to be in the best interest of whites over any other nationality. In this way, the oppression of others is inevitable because it has to be. There can be no sustaining of white power without the task of oppressing others.

In acknowledging the socioeconomic issues raised in the music of Akrobatik, his message of equity and fair treatment must not be forgotten as it stands on the foundation of a socioeconomic theology established long ago. It was Christ who came not only preaching a message of salvation and reconciliation to God, but he likewise preached a gospel that advocated for the least, lost, and left out. Akrobatik briefly gives voice to the external socioeconomic insecurities of the black community before he sheds light on the internal struggles that aid in the disparities of the black community.

> It makes me wonder how a black man could ever raise a child out here. . .remind my soul.

---

8. Irons, *White Men's Law*, i.

Though these issues are applicable throughout the United States, this work is written specifically through the lens of one who sees first-hand the socioeconomic struggles of black Americans in Boston, Massachusetts. These issues of socioeconomics were not simply the reality of Akrobatik's generation. Prior to the early 2000s and as early as the first arrival of blacks to Boston in 1638, blacks have consistently lived through the torture and economic poverty of raising families in Boston. It was not simply about being able to raise a child in Boston but if blacks would be able to *survive* Boston.

Considering the post-slavery history of blacks in Boston, it is important to recognize that although many blacks fled to Boston from the southern United States, it did not mean that blacks were absolved of socioeconomic issues that would plague the community then as they do now. "The decisive events in the South encouraged activists all across the United States to intensify the ongoing struggles for equality and justice in their own respective local communities. Black Bostonians were no exception."[9] So many do not "understand that Northern states were pioneers in disenfranchising free Blacks and in developing customs and laws that racially segregated public transportation, neighborhoods, and jobs even before the Civil War."[10]

These laws did not go unnoticed or unchallenged. The first documented act of resistance is credited to Frederick Douglass and James Buffum in 1841. "On September 29, 1841, Fredrick Douglass and his friend James N. Buffum protested due to the fact that they were not allowed to travel in first class with white passengers on the Eastern Railroad Company."[11] Only five days after this incident, Douglass would give a speech in Hingham, Massachusetts, that spoke to the actual evil for which resistance was required. The speech, entitled "The Church and Prejudice," "criticized ministers who used the Bible to defend slavery,"[12] and the ensuing marginalizations that would come as a result of their defense of slavery. For Douglas, prejudice goes even into the church of God. He suggested, "There are those who carry it so far that it is disagreeable to them even to think of going to heaven if colored people are going there too . . . the grand cause is slavery."[13]

---

9. Dunham, "Boston's 1960s Civil Rights Movement," para. 5.

10. Davis, "Black Freedom Struggle of the North," para. 3.

11. Lauranzano, "Resistance to the Segregation of Public Transportation in the Early 1840s," para. 2.

12. Hingham Unity Council, "1841," para. 1.

13. Hingham Unity Council, "1841," para. 4.

## Part Two: Response

Still, there is an interesting metamorphosis of events involving transportation in Boston. More recently and as late as the 1970s, the city of Boston still practiced segregation in plain view. They did so through their school systems, where students were intentionally segregated based on where they lived. Ultimately, this practice forced the government to get involved, and "busing" became the response. A governmental response to socioeconomic oppression created a firestorm of responses from both whites and blacks in Boston. "The truth is that 65 years after the Supreme Court struck down school segregation in Brown v. Board of Education, black children are as segregated from white students as they were in the mid-1970s"[14] in the city of Boston. An attempt to desegregate Boston's schools became an intense time in the city. A court-ordered decision drew criticism from the advantaged and the oppressed.

Opposition to busing in Boston was not simply a white issue, but it also raised issues among blacks in Boston. Notable figures such as Louise Day Hicks were among those who led anti-busing protests and fought against the system of busing in Boston. In this, "the question remains whether or not busing served its purpose of breaking apart the educational caste system."[15] The reality is that it may no longer be a busing system that haunts the Boston community, but as it is in other cities, students are still segregated by other socioeconomic systems of oppression.

Not only does the history of blacks in Boston include the issue of busing, but blacks also face external opposition via housing discrimination. By 1978, blacks in Chelsea, Massachusetts, and Boston, Massachusetts, had grown more weary of their cities' treatment and decided to pursue litigation.

> On April 17, 1978, two citizens of Massachusetts filed lawsuits under the Housing and Community Development Act of 1977 against the Department of Housing and Urban Development (HUD) in the U.S. District Court for the District of Massachusetts. The plaintiffs, represented by the National Association for the Advancement of Colored People (NAACP), alleged that their constitutional rights had been violated by racially discriminatory disbursement of federal housing funds in the cities of Boston and Chelsea.[16]

---

14. Hannah-Jones, "It Was Never About Busing," para. 3.
15. Hannah-Jones, "It Was Never About Busing," para. 3.
16. "NAACP, Boston Chapter v. HUD," para. 1.

The black experience in 1960s Boston and Chelsea included discriminatory practices when black people attempted to secure shelter in private and public places of housing. As one of the most vulnerable communities within Boston, blacks were intentionally marginalized through unfair qualification criteria, unfair rates for blacks to which other races were not subject. This made the black community even more vulnerable because it limited access to equitable housing. "As of September 1, 1963, of the 25 public housing projects operated by the Boston Housing Authority, seventeen had less than five percent Negro families, and in six projects totaling 2,888 family units, there were no Negro families. Four projects were more than 90 percent Negro and were rapidly approaching the 100 percent mark."[17]

With the aforementioned socioeconomic issue very much at play, there is no way to ignore or omit how housing discrimination contributes to poverty in black communities, especially seen in Boston. These issues inundate the poetic concerns within Akrobatik's music. The domino effect of socioeconomic oppression perpetuates poverty, and poverty perpetuates crime. "America has historically had a poor habit of redirecting blame for substandard schools, low wages, and scarcity of jobs away from the structural forces that caused these problems while simultaneously reinforcing negative stereotypes about African American families."[18]

Twenty-first century Boston knows the weight of poverty that resulted in crime as well. One report states, "At least 21.6% of Boston's population lives in poverty. This percentage has remained fairly consistent since 2000. In comparison, the U.S. poverty rate [at this time] is 15.9%, and the Massachusetts poverty rate is 11.9%. . . . Poverty rates are higher for Boston's Hispanic, Asian, and Black/African American populations, and lowest for Boston's White population. Poverty rates according to race are . . . Black/African American: 23%."[19] The disproportionate nature of poverty in Boston is proof of socioeconomic systems that cater to one group and oppress others. In that oppression, basic human rights are often violated. As has been true internationally and domestically, local to Boston, chronic illness, high mortality rates, and mental illness are just a few of the symptoms of poverty.

With the prevalence of poverty also comes the presence of crime. The statistics of crime in Boston, as in other cities, are not always fairly

---

17. *Discrimination in Housing in the Boston Metropolitan Area*, 10.
18. Greenbaum, *Blaming the Poor*, 2.
19. Boston Redevelopment Authority Research Division, *Poverty in Boston*, 4–5.

reported. These statistics suggest that differences in neighborhood reporting trends exist for robbery and assault but not for homicide. Specifically, "The news media tend to disproportionately report more robberies and assaults in neighborhoods with lower levels of neighborhood disadvantage. Implications for the social construction of crime and neighborhoods, as well as criminal justice response for disadvantaged neighborhoods, are discussed."[20] The disproportionate media coverage is not surprising considering the sanitization of white crime for the preservation of white power; meanwhile, minorities are often rightfully or wrongfully convicted of crimes, and their convictions are brought to national display to shame them while "informing" others.

> Will they get programmed how to behave?
> Malcolm X must be turnin' in his grave

Though there were celebrations of a decline in crime, this decline gave rise to an increase in other areas, and Boston has certainly felt that reality. According to the *Boston Review*,

> By the early 2000s incarceration rates had grown to extraordinary levels in poor communities. Whole generations of young, mostly minority and poorly educated men were being locked up, leading to the United States's current status as the world's largest jailer, in both absolute and relative terms. Prisons may have reduced crime a little in the short run, but at the current scale the negative effects of incarceration are likely to outweigh the positive. Commonplace incarceration among poor young men fuels cynicism about the legal system, destabilizes families, and reduces economic opportunities.[21]

Certainly, external systems of oppression have been just as powerful as internal systems of crisis within the Boston community. Akrobatik speaks of his concern about the incarceration of blacks that attempts to or successfully de-programs blacks of the legacy of their ancestors. The system(s) in place programs some blacks to a new reality that demonizes their blackness. America has created a system that dismisses the truth of a culture and body of people who were and still are highly intellectual, kings and queens in this world.

---

20. Baranauskas, "Exploring the Social Construction of Crime by Neighborhood," 156.

21. Western, "Crime and Punishment," paras. 4–5.

## SOCIOECONOMIC THEOLOGY ON THE MIC

The necessity of a socioeconomic theology is how the soul is reminded and ultimately encouraged. The message of Akrobatik reflects the language of socioeconomic theology, and the soul is reminded of the words of Jesus in Matthew's Gospel. The most vulnerable, the poor, and the marginalized are of great concert to Jesus. For Jesus, service to the least of these is a service to him. Jesus says, "And the King will answer them, 'Truly, I say to you, as you did it to one of the least of these my brothers, you did it to me.'"[22]

The socioeconomic welfare of human creation has always been important to God. In Christ's thirty-three years on this earth, he spent much of his ministry addressing issues dealing with poverty, the oppressed, and the neglected. Consider the socioeconomic status of the Savior born into the world he made. Christ is not conceived in the womb of a woman with powerful prowess, nor is he cared for at the hands of a man of great political or social authority. Mary and Joseph, according to Scripture, "Went up from Galilee, from the town of Nazareth, to Judea, to the city of David, which is called Bethlehem . . . and while they were there, the time came for her to give birth. And she gave birth to her firstborn son and wrapped him in swaddling clothes and laid him in a manger because there was no place for them in the inn."[23] The baby, "so holy, meek yet so mild,"[24] comes to this earth, and his socioeconomic status immediately mirrors "the least of these."

Some have argued that the "lowly" environment of Christ's birth is purely circumstantial. Jason Osai, in his article entitled "Jesus: Born Poor or Rich?," suggests,

> Biblical accounts indicate that when Joseph arrived at Bethlehem for the census, he went from one inn to another in search for room to lodge with his pregnant wife but was not able to find one on account of the fact that all the inns were fully booked; this phenomenon is common till date: when major events take place in cities, the hospitality industry is usually overstretched and the hotels are generally fully booked except for those who made reservations. This therefore means that the birth of Jesus in a manger where animals are kept was circumstantial: it was predicated on the non-availability of accommodation at the inns rather than the issue of non-affordability or poverty. Joseph Carpenter had enough money

---

22. Matt 25:40 ESV.
23. Luke 2:4–7 ESV.
24. Allison, "Glory, Glory to the Newborn King."

to pay for a space in an inn and searched extensively for one but could not find so, out of frustration and shire [sic] necessity or Divine design, he resorted to a manger.[25]

This moment could be seen as circumstantial, but it likewise speaks to the sovereignty of God and the example of Christ. Christ would have retained his divine nature regardless of whether he was born in an inn or a stable. However, it is significant that God intentionally chose for Christ's birth to mirror the socioeconomic conditions that those who would come to know him would experience. The experience is a reality marked by struggle. The witness of Christ is acquainted with the suffering. The suffering Savior, "a man of sorrows acquainted with grief,"[26] is also acquainted with those who are oppressed. He is the "God of the oppressed—on the side of the oppressed."[27] Howard Thurman makes this clear in his description of Jesus. As One who is on the side of the oppressed, he is well-acquainted with oppression and those who are oppressed. Howard Thurman notes, "We begin with the simple historical fact that Jesus was a Jew . . . the second important fact for our consideration is that he was a poor Jew. . . . The economic predicament with which he was identified in birth placed him initially with the great mass of men on the earth. The masses of the people are poor. . . . The third fact is that Jesus was a member of a minority group in the midst of a larger dominant and controlling group."[28]

The divinity of the infant Christ is not at risk because of his socioeconomic standing. For Thurman, "If we dare take the position that in Jesus there was at work some radical destiny, it would be safe to say that in his poverty he was more truly Son of man than he would have been if the incident of family or birth had made him a rich son of Israel."[29] He has simply been born into a system where socioeconomic standards determine the manner in which he will be viewed and treated. This predetermined social hierarchy is a reflection of Akrobatik's initial question, "How can a black man raise a child out here?"[30] Socioeconomic standards were prede-

---

25. Osai, "Jesus," 223.

26. Isa 53:3 ESV.

27. This is in reference to the originally published 1975 work by James Cone entitled *God of the Oppressed*. In this work, Cone discusses liberation at the intersection of Christianity and the oppression of black communities in America.

28. Thurman, *Jesus and the Disinherited*, 5–8.

29. Thurman, *Jesus and the Disinherited*, 7.

30. Akrobatik, "Remind My Soul."

termined for blacks in America by those who sought majority and primary power by any means necessary—even via slavery. The humanity of blacks in America has constantly dealt with threats just as Christ dealt with threats to his humanity. America, as ancient Nazareth was for Joseph, Mary, and Christ, was not and has not been a safe place for the oppressed.

> My elders all feel the same there's no bravery
> We're supposed to fight for freedom not just the end of slavery . . .

Ultimately, Akrobatik raises a holy concern on behalf of blacks in Boston and around the domestic United States. Liberation theology shares a similar concern. The concern is that liberation and the road to socioeconomic equity is not simply in freedom from the chains of slavery by external oppressors, but there must be a longing for freedom amid the black community where black minds are free and desire to fight for more.

In the liberation theology movement, Gustavo Gutiérrez, among others, would agree that the external issues must also be addressed. Emerging in the 1950s, the liberation theology movement primarily sought to address the church's action and inaction when it came to those who were in poverty and experienced oppression. "The gap between the rich and poor nations and peoples is increasingly widening. These developments have led to the virtual disappearance of the middle class, which has plunged into poverty. It has given rise to what has been called 'neo-dualism': the population is ever increasingly polarised at the two extremes of the social and economic spectrum."[31]

For Gutiérrez (just as for Frederick Douglass), the church has participated in the oppression, socioeconomic or otherwise, of others—and Jesus and Paul would likely hold the same position. Instead of continuing the charge to "preach the gospel to the poor," like the Sadducees in Acts 5, church leaders in powerful positions attempted to silence the hopes of the poor and physically abused them for maintaining hope of the resurrected Savior and a brighter future that awaited them, so they arrested the disciples for preaching the good news to the poor. Like the Sadducees, the Pharisees knew the law and used the same law to oppress others. Jesus describes the keepers of the law/religious leaders:

> The Scribes and the Pharisees sit on Moses' seat, so do and observe whatever they tell you, but not the works they do. For they preach, but do not practice. They tie up heavy burdens, hard to bear, and

---

31. Gutiérrez and Condor, "Task and Content of Liberation Theology," 23.

> lay them on people's shoulders, but they themselves are not willing to move them with their finger. "But woe to you, scribes and Pharisees, hypocrites! For you shut the kingdom of heaven in people's faces. For you neither enter yourselves nor allow those who would enter to go in. Woe to you, scribes and Pharisees, hypocrites! For you travel across sea and land to make a single proselyte, and when he becomes a proselyte, you make him twice as much a child of hell as yourselves.[32]

For this reason, God sends Jesus as the fulfillment of the law, and thus commences the hatred or the despising of Jesus by these religious persons.

The hypocrisy of the church becomes localized for Akrobatik in the city of Boston. In 2014, the Anti-Racism Team (ART) of Trinity Church Boston completed the necessary work of acknowledging and atoning for their past—their participation in systems of oppression that directly impacted the lives of people of color in Boston. Their truth is that their church has unfortunately and often perpetuated the oppression from which Jesus sought to free all of human creation.

> Therefore, in the following document, we focus on times when individual racial prejudice becomes linked to systems and institutions of power in a way that gives advantages to the dominant group over others. In the American colonies and then in the United States, systems of power were and are often stacked to give advantage to white people at the expense of other racial groups. This is what is described by the term "White privilege." We seek to identify instances of that occurring in the history of Trinity Church.
>
> The Episcopal Church in the United States of America has undertaken similar efforts with Pastoral Letters of March 1994 and March 2006 on the Sin of Racism and with resolutions passed at its General Conventions of 2006, 2009, and 2012, calling for each diocese to gather information in its own community on (1) the complicity of the Episcopal Church in the institution of slavery and in the subsequent history of segregation and discrimination; (2) examples of resistance to slavery and discrimination; and (3) the economic benefits derived by the Episcopal Church from the transatlantic slave trade and the institution of slavery.[33]

Theologian James Cone would agree with Christ, Gutiérrez, and the ART of Trinity Church Boston.

---

32. Matt 23:3–5, 13–15 ESV.
33. Soussou et al., "Trinity Church of Boston."

> The Church has a responsibility to participate in the liberation of all oppressed people as it is itself a product of liberation. Still, history and our present often remind us that the Church has failed to do so. If the real Church is the people of God whose primary task is that of being Christ to the world by proclaiming the message of the gospel, by rendering services of liberation, and by being itself a manifestation of the nature of the new society, then the empirical institutionalized white church has failed on all counts. The church has certainly not rendered services of reconciliation to the poor. Rather, the church in America displays the values of a sick society that oppresses the poor.[34]

"People are becoming aware that this liberation implies a break with the status quo, and that it calls for a social revolution."[35] In the opening verse of his song, Akrobatik addresses what has been described through the lens of Scripture, the experience of Gutiérrez, and the witness of Cone: the legacy of the United States as a country built on the successful and sustained oppression of other peoples. The listener is reminded of the horrors of a nation that plagued generations of blacks and why socioeconomic theology, through the lens of liberation theology, is a necessary witness in this world.

## ENGAGING IN THE INNER WORK

> We're taught to worship these rappers and athletes and actors
> Many who think they better and they walk right past ya . . .

Akrobatik makes a shift from the external issues plaguing the black community in Boston to the internal issues that plague the black community. In the bar above, Akrobatik discusses the dismissive nature of those within his community who are revered by the people but are ignored by those they idolize simultaneously. Though in different economic and social classes, the gesture of the successful to ignore those of lower classes is harmful especially within the same community—more specifically, the black community. Akrobatik suggests that Arthur Ashe did not achieve success then dismiss those of the community to which he belonged. As the first and (still) only black man to win Wimbledon and the U.S. Open tennis championships, Arthur Ashe made significant contributions to the black community while

---

34. Cone, *Black Theology and Black Power*, 71.
35. Gutiérrez, *Theology of Liberation*, 59.

## Part Two: Response

being committed to raising awareness concerning AIDS. His achievements benefited others especially in his own community. Akrobatik raises Arthur Ashe as one who would not participate in ignoring his own community as a result of success. The overarching idea is that Arthur Ashe remained connected and concerned about his community despite his titles, his success, and even the power that came with money, titles, and success.

The disciples' journeys mirror the overarching idea of remaining connected to the community even with power and titles. An incident in Acts 3 comes to mind:

> Now Peter and John were going up to the temple at the hour of prayer, the ninth hour. And a man lame from birth was being carried, whom they laid daily at the gate of the temple that is called the Beautiful Gate to ask alms of those entering the temple. Seeing Peter and John about to go into the temple, he asked to receive alms. And Peter directed his gaze at him, as did John, and said, "Look at us." And he fixed his attention on them, expecting to receive something from them. But Peter said, "I have no silver and gold, but what I do have I give to you. In the name of Jesus Christ of Nazareth, rise up and walk!" And he took him by the right hand and raised him up, and immediately his feet and ankles were made strong. And leaping up, he stood and began to walk, and entered the temple with them, walking and leaping and praising God. And all the people saw him walking and praising God, and recognized him as the one who sat at the Beautiful Gate of the temple, asking for alms. And they were filled with wonder and amazement at what had happened to him.[36]

Essentially, Peter and John meet a man at a gate that others walk through on their way to prayer. The man is in financial despair and paralytic but is at the gate asking for alms. Peter and John, when spotted by the man and asked, respond that they do not have what he is asking for, but what they do have is the name that they carry. They offer that name to the man, and subsequently, because of the man's faith, he is healed in the name of Jesus. The man responds in joy, and it is made visible to all who are near.

It is clear that the emphasis of this miracle lies in the name of Jesus. This passage in Acts 3 highlights the power of Jesus' name, as it has power that no other name has. Jesus began his ministry by manifesting the healing power of God's rule to the amazement of all; now we see that Peter and the apostles carry on the same work with the same power. "By faith in

---

36. Acts 3:1–10 ESV.

his name, this name has made this [lame] man strong" (Acts 3:16).[37] The name of Christ does more than the alms the man had already been given and could have been given in his encounter with Peter and John. Beyond the immediate desire of the man, he receives what he needs because of this moment.

The focal point of this passage is the power of Jesus' name, but underneath this point is an indictment on those who neglect the poor. For context, "By the time of Acts 3, the apostolic church was growing and was beginning to challenge the municipal aristocracy (the political elite)."[38] In this passage, the impact of apostolic leadership and humility amidst the community is emphasized. The disciples' positions as apostles being coupled with humility is important because the setting of this passage finds the man at the gate that leads to a temple at the time of prayer. "Daily prayer and poverty were located in the same place."[39]

The man is unable to walk but is brought to the temple gate, where prayer is offered. He is left to advocate for himself in his condition. Many people in ancient times were stigmatized because of their physical ailments or differences. For many of them, they did not simply deal with the pain of their condition, but they also dealt with the prejudices of their communities. Before Jesus heals a man born blind, this very stigma and prejudice presents itself in Scripture. As he passed by, he saw a man blind from birth. And his disciples asked him, "Rabbi, who sinned, this man or his parents, that he was born blind?" Jesus answered, "It was not that this man sinned, or his parents, but that the works of God might be displayed in him."[40] In the same way that a stigma is placed on the blind man, it is not far-fetched that the man at the gate would have experienced the same.

> It's what you do off camera and off the court
> That really makes you worthy of the people support.

The man is brought to the gate but never taken into the temple. He is obviously in need of assistance but his need limits his access to the temple. Perhaps, in his experience, his most immediate help was outside of the temple versus inside. The man brought to the gate encounters several people who could assist him outside the gate but is not invited beyond the

---

37. Brown, *Introduction to the New Testament*, 290.
38. Keener, *Acts*, 179.
39. Keener, *Acts*, 182.
40. John 9:1–3 ESV.

## Part Two: Response

gate—but there is ministry at the gate. Those who are on their way to prayer are engaging in the vertical work of ministering to God (through prayer) which should prompt them to the horizontal work of ministering to their fellow man by way of service to humanity. Still, this man sits at the gate.

In the aforementioned passage, there are faith leaders and others within the community of believers who have risen to power and prominence or have been appointed to high positions, and it seems as if they have forgotten the assignment of service to others—especially to those who are the poorest and most vulnerable amongst them. They've risen to these positions and suddenly, they've forgotten Akrobatik alludes to a similar concern in the fifth stanza of his song concerning the black community's internal struggles:

> But some brothers get those millions and forget how to behave
> Arthur Ashe must be turnin' in his grave.

Akrobatik suggests that brothers within the black community (sisters not to be exempt from this) have achieved levels of success that they may have never dreamed. The success of those (within the black community) who acquire millions, high positions and power is not the issue; the real issue is who they become as a result of their success and positions. He asserts that they have gotten the millions, the success, but have forgotten the most important work within the black community. This is the same issue we see amongst those who enter the temple to pray but ignore those in need who sit just at the temple's gate. These are Jews and high priests who go through the gates to enter the temple. They are headed to pray, but somehow miss the ministry that meets them before prayer, via those who sit at the gate and cannot enter. They are dressed for worship in the temple but dismiss the ministry to their community. These persons who are able to enter the temple and even the high priests are essentially dressed for church and walking by ministry. To have made it to a certain level within one's community but consciously choose to ignore those suffering within the community is an unrighteous action. Peter and John do not claim to possess the riches or the social elitism of this Jewish community, but they do share that name which has the power to make this man whole.

In the final verse of his song, Akrobatik addresses the worth placed on wealth within the black community:

> We crabs in a barrel, you ain't getting out until I do first ...
> Whatever happened to strength in numbers?

He references the mentality that suggests "If I cannot do it, you cannot do it either." This attitude is jealousy and dysfunctional when the reality is that everyone within the community needs assistance. So dysfunctional is the thought that Akrobatik has experienced those willing to kill others simply to stop them from experiencing life beyond where they are. He asks the question, "Whatever happened to strength in numbers?" It's a holy question, and its practice is reflected in the Scriptures.

Second Corinthians 8 contains a passage where the concept of strength in numbers is fully displayed.

> We want you to know, brothers, about the grace of God that has been given among the churches of Macedonia, for in a severe test of affliction, their abundance of joy and their extreme poverty have overflowed in a wealth of generosity on their part. For they gave according to their means, as I can testify, and beyond their means, of their own accord, begging us earnestly for the favor of taking part in the relief of the saints—and this, not as we expected, but they gave themselves first to the Lord and then by the will of God to us. Accordingly, we urged Titus that as he had started, so he should complete among you this act of grace. But as you excel in everything—in faith, in speech, in knowledge, in all earnestness, and in our love for you—see that you excel in this act of grace also.[41]

The passage calls the reader to examine their motive for giving. As described in the text, the brothers and sisters in Macedonia do not all give only out of lack or only out of abundance. Each of them is giving to someone else according to their means and even beyond their means—for the sake of someone else's welfare. There is a collective effort to ensure that another group of believers is cared for by positively addressing their economic welfare. Paul writes such a request to the Corinthians giving the example of the Macedonian Christians, who are being generous despite their poverty, as well as that of Jesus Christ himself, "who, though he was rich, for our sake became poor, that you might become rich by his poverty."[42]

Collective strength is on display by the Macedonian Christians; through the generosity of those who lived in abundance and those who did not, the care for all in Jerusalem is taken seriously. They also were not coerced into generosity by the promise of being financially reimbursed for their kindness. The collective strength and kindness of the Macedonian

---

41. 2 Cor 8:1–7 ESV.

42. Brown, *Introduction to the New Testament*, 546.

## Part Two: Response

Christian community is not the "crabs in a barrel" mentality Akrobatik saw within the black community. This response to the economic reality of those in Jerusalem causes Paul to commend the Macedonians for their work and use their work as an example to the church at Corinth of what it looks like to work together to see others in a better socioeconomic reality. As a church and as a community, they addressed the needs of others.

As it relates to the theme of internal and external socioeconomic issues being addressed in the black community, there is a tone of hopeful skepticism throughout Akrobatik's "Remind My Soul." His posture in the song is based on the history of his environment and his experiences. There is indeed a remnant of the black community who are integrally addressing these issues. All of these issues will not immediately be resolved in their totality, but every person who desires to do the work of rebuilding and rebranding within the black community has an opportunity to be a part of the work. There is more than enough that plagues the black community from the outside that includes systemic oppression from Americans and those around the world who already view blacks as less than. According to Akrobatik, there is then certainly no room for hate within the black community. The necessity for solidarity and mindfulness in the black community is not an option. Akrobatik is akin to Solomon, who, long before, wrote, "Two are better than one, because they have a good reward for their toil. For if they fall, one will lift up his fellow. But woe to him who is alone when he falls and has not another to lift him up! Again, if two lie together, they keep warm, but how can one keep warm alone? And though a man might prevail against one who is alone, two will withstand him—a threefold cord is not quickly broken."[43]

## BIBLIOGRAPHY

Akrobatik. "Remind My Soul." 2003. https://genius.com/Akrobatik-remind-my-soul-lyrics.

Allison, Margaret. "Glory, Glory to the Newborn King." Hymnary, 1950. https://hymnary.org/text/jesus_jesus_oh_what_a_wonderful_child.

Baranauskas, Andrew J. "Exploring the Social Construction of Crime by Neighborhood: News Coverage of Crime in Boston." *Sociological Focus* 53 (2020) 156–76.

Boston Redevelopment Authority Research Division. *Poverty in Boston.* Mar. 2014. https://www.bostonplans.org/getattachment/f1ecaf8a-d529-40b6-a9bc-8b4419587b86.

Brown, Raymond E. *An Introduction to the New Testament.* New York: Doubleday, 1997.

Cone, James H. *Black Theology and Black Power.* Maryknoll, NY: Orbis, 2018.

43. Eccl 4:9–12 ESV.

Davis, Joshua Clark. "The Black Freedom Struggle of the North." African American Intellectual Historical Society, Aug. 20, 2020. https://www.aaihs.org/the-black-freedom-struggle-of-the-north/.

*Discrimination in Housing in the Boston Metropolitan Area; Report.* District of Columbia, 1963.

Dunham, Audrea F. Jones. "Boston's 1960s Civil Rights Movement: A Look Back." GBH Openvault, n.d. https://openvault.wgbh.org/exhibits/boston_civil_rights/article.

Greenbaum, Susan D. *Blaming the Poor: The Long Shadow of the Moynihan Report on Cruel Images About Poverty.* New Brunswick, NJ: Rutgers University Press, 2015. https://doi.org/10.2307/j.ctt15sk7xn.

Gutiérrez, Gustavo. *A Theology of Liberation.* Maryknoll, NY: Orbis, 1988.

Gutiérrez, G., and Judith Condor. "The Task and Content of Liberation Theology." In *The Cambridge Companion to Liberation Theology*, edited by Christopher Rowland, 19–38. Cambridge: Cambridge University Press, 2007.

Hannah-Jones, Nikole. "It Was Never About Busing." *The New York Times*, July 12, 2019. https://www.nytimes.com/2019/07/12/opinion/sunday/it-was-never-about-busing.html.

Hingham Unity Council. "1841: Frederick Douglass Delivers One of His First Recorded Anti-Slavery Speeches in Hingham." Jan. 23, 2021. https://hinghamunity.org/1841-frederick-douglass-speech/.

Horton, Carol A. *Race and the Making of American Liberalism.* Oxford: Oxford University Press, 2005.

Irons, Peter H. *White Men's Law: The Roots of Systemic Racism.* New York: Oxford University Press, 2022.

Keener, Craig S. *Acts.* New Cambridge Bible Commentary. Cambridge: Cambridge University Press, 2020.

King, Martin Luther, Jr. "Letter from Birmingham Jail." 1963. https://www.csuchico.edu/iege/_assets/documents/susi-letter-from-birmingham-jail.pdf.

Lauranzano, Peter. "Resistance to the Segregation of Public Transportation in the Early 1840s." Primary Research, Mar. 10, 2009. https://primaryresearch.org/resistance-to-the-segregation-of-public-transportation-in-the-early-1840s/.

"NAACP, Boston Chapter v. HUD 1:78-Cv-00850 (D.Mass.)." Civil Rights Litigation Clearinghouse, Apr. 17, 1978. https://clearinghouse.net/case/5496/.

Nellis, Ashley. "The Color of Justice: Racial and Ethnic Disparity in State Prisons." The Sentencing Project, Oct. 13, 2021. https://www.sentencingproject.org/reports/the-color-of-justice-racial-and-ethnic-disparity-in-state-prisons-the-sentencing-project/.

Njoku, Anuli, et al. "Listen to the Whispers Before They Become Screams: Addressing Black Maternal Morbidity and Mortality in the United States." *Healthcare* 11 (2023) 438. https://doi.org/10.3390/healthcare11030438.

Osai, Jason. "Jesus: Born Poor or Rich?" *African Research Review* 7 (2013) 217–31.

Soussou, Helen, et al. "Trinity Church Boston: Facing the Reality of Our Past." Accessed February 20, 2024. https://www.trinitychurchboston.org/sites/default/files/ART_History_Book_0.pdf.

Thurman, Howard. *Jesus and the Disinherited.* Boston: Beacon, 1976.

Western, Bruce. "Crime and Punishment: Public Safety Doesn't Require More Inmates." *Boston Review*, Mar. 1, 2012. https://www.bostonreview.net/articles/bruce-western-crime-rate-prison-population-america/.

Wilkerson, Isabel. *Caste: The Origins of Our Discontent.* New York: Random House, 2023.

# 6

# The Voice of Wisdom Cries Out
*Poetic, Prophetic Proverbs*

### Alex Sosler

Wisdom cries aloud in the street,
    in the markets she raises her voice;
at the head of the noisy streets she cries out;
    at the entrance of the city gates she speaks:
"How long, O simple ones, will you love being simple?
How long will scoffers delight in their scoffing
    and fools hate knowledge?"

—Proverbs 1:20–22 (ESV throughout)

To know wisdom and instruction,
    to understand words of insight,
  to receive instruction in wise dealing,
    in righteousness, justice, and equity;
  to give prudence to the simple,
    knowledge and discretion to the youth—
Let the wise hear and increase in learning,

# The Voice of Wisdom Cries Out—Sosler

> and the one who understands obtain guidance,
> to understand a proverb and a saying,
> the words of the wise and their riddles.
> The fear of the LORD is the beginning of knowledge;
> fools despise wisdom and instruction.
>
> —Proverbs 1:2–7

I GREW UP IN Cleveland, Ohio. I'm not East Coast or West Coast. I'm Midwest. Perhaps more properly, I'm from a "flyover" state. (Sadly, people do not usually take vacations to come visit Ohio.) The Midwest didn't invent social consciousness in the rap game, but they have specialized in it—think Cleveland's Bone Thugs-N-Harmony or Chicago's Common and Lupe Fiasco. Being from the Midwest, I'm drawn to this Midwest consciousness. To be fair, I'm a fan of party anthems as well. Having been raised on the east side of Cleveland, I'll claim Kid Cudi and Machine Gun Kelly without hesitation. But there's something entrenched about the social consciousness that rap often carries.

I resonate with Rick Ross's critique about the current commercialization of rap: "It's all about packaging and marketing. Talent is no longer a requirement. Sources like BET, MTV, MySpace, and others dictate who will make it and who will fail."[1] Here's the problem when all becomes subject to packaging and marketing: virtue seldom sells. For hip-hop in Atlanta, the market research is done in strip clubs (not exactly a paradigm of wisdom). The challenge for hip-hoppers is learning how to make the harmful things uncool and virtuous things cool.[2]

RZA, a founding member of Wu-Tang Clan, also identifies this problem. In an interview with the *Washington Post* in 2022, he comments, "The wisdom is missing. Sometimes people think hip-hop is just about money,

---

1. Quoted in Hodge, *Soul of Hip Hop*, 117. The phenomena of the rapper "6ix9ine" could be an extreme example. Basically, his main goal was to go viral, so he used whatever means necessary to be famous. It worked, but I'm not sure it was good for the world or his own soul.

2. Referenced in Fiasco, "Rap Theory and Practice." Unfortunately, in art of all sorts, virtue is boring. In everything from the television series *Breaking Bad* to rap music, badness is more entertaining, often more compelling, than goodness. There are rare instances where virtue is interesting. (See Bilbro, "Taste of Strawberries," on how Tolkien makes virtue interesting.)

drugs and sex and good times. And that's just one pillar. Where's the pillar of information? Where's the pillar of inspiration? And I don't mean inspiration to want to go out on Saturday and party. But inspiration that even another artist can hear, and a painter can listen to and paint his greatest painting because of the poetical words that's passing through his mind. Where's that at? Those things have been removed, or there's less of it because of the popularity of it has dwindled."[3] Wisdom inspires, yet sometimes rap plays to our basic and easy instincts.

The journalist and linguist John McWhorter once wrote that rap retards black success.[4] While one can be sympathetic with the critique—there tends to be a glorification of violence, sex, and vain pursuits—I think he's wrong. You could make a case if you ignore all lyrics except the controversial ones. But I think we should judge hip-hop by its best lyrics rather than its worst. There may always be a shade cast over hip-hop due to the historical judgment, but it also shines light in its dark places. Hip-hop has a long history where artists envision a different and wiser future. They speak of their experience because that's what they know. But they also have an imagination to see their way out.

In a lecture at the Massachusetts Institute of Technology, Lupe Fiasco argues that rap has an inherent teaching purpose.[5] Rap teaches listeners how to dress, what to believe, and how to go to jail, he suggests. Fiasco wants to introduce a new form, a new teaching. Can hip-hop orient listeners to different goals and different beliefs? Can hip-hop introduce a new imagination?

In the book of Proverbs, wisdom is compared to a voice that cries out in a busy street and asks, "How long, O simple ones, will you love being simple? How long will scoffers delight in their scoffing and fools hate knowledge?" (Prov 1:20–21). After a brief discussion on the nature and purpose of Proverbs, I'll present how a few contemporary commentators shout in a simple world. Houston's Tobe Nwigwe, Chicago's Chance the Rapper, and Atlanta's Killer Mike are the main dialogue partners.[6]

3. Otteson, "RZA on the Current State of Hip Hop."
4. McWhorter, "How Hip-Hop Holds Blacks Back."
5. See Fiasco, "Rap Theory and Practice." Perhaps more pointedly, W. E. B. Du Bois argued that all art is propaganda, stating, "I do not care a damn for any art that is not used for propaganda. But I do care when propaganda is confined to one side while the other is stripped and silent." Du Bois, "Criteria for Negro Art."
6. I'll be using some of their most recent albums. For Tobe, *moMINTS* (2022) and *CINCORIGINALS* (2020). For Chance the Rapper, *The Big Day* (2019). For Killer Mike,

## THE PURPOSE AND NATURE OF WISDOM

> The beginning of wisdom is this: Get wisdom, and whatever you get, get insight.
> —Proverbs 4:7

Wisdom encompasses a whole genre of biblical literature. According to biblical scholar Raymond Van Leeuwen, wisdom is "a totalizing concept that seeks to bring all of life's activities into harmony with God's created order."[7] God created the world in a certain way. By observing the laws of nature, cause and effect, and order, one can ascertain certain truths about life and the best way to live. The wise seek to conform to this wisdom embedded in the world.

Bruce Waltke and Ivan de Silva see this vision of wisdom as limited. They suggest that the author of Proverbs, for example, does not base their reflections on natural theology; rather, "they view all creation and all human activity through the lens of faith in Israel's covenant-keeping God. Without this point of view, observing nature could teach the 'law of survival of the fittest' and not the way of righteousness, leading them to commend the use of power and dominance."[8] In other words, if you look at the world for wisdom, you may not find it. Concerning hip-hop, looking at the street corner for wisdom may lead you down a vice-ridden path. The nature of what one observes may be misleading. It seems like evil prospers sometimes (reading Job or certain Psalms, for example).

So, hip-hop needs divinely inspired imaginers. Proverbs are more than bland advice-giving; rather, proverbs are world-creating. It's a way of seeing the world. Imagining a better future is a key feature of the black experience. The African American novelist Kaitlyn Greenidge connects this vision to slave spirituals through emancipation, imagining an unknowable future. "We are champion imaginers," she writes, "usually thinking of things ten, twenty, one hundred years beyond what our masters, captors, police and jailers ever could. When I listen to and read about the old spirituals now, I understand them to be maps of profound imagination."[9] While I do not mean to suggest that hip-hop artists provide wisdom "through the lens of faith in Israel's covenant-keeping God," hip-hop artists do provide a greater

---

*MICHAEL* (2023).

7. Van Leeuwen, "Wisdom Literature," 847.
8. Waltke and de Silva, *Proverbs*, 16–17.
9. Greenidge, "Black Spirituals as Poetry and Resistance," 17.

Part Two: Response

frame to view life. They can offer an alternative imagination to the contemporary world. There's a prophetic wisdom they offer. There is power in offering wisdom, as the beginning of Prov 2 points out. For those who seek wisdom and treasure instruction and incline their heart to understanding will find the knowledge of God (Prov 2:1–5). The search for wisdom ends in the face of Jesus Christ. So, while hip-hop's proverbs may have limits, they set the direction correctly. There is blessing, pleasantness, and rest in the life of wisdom (Prov 3:13–18).

In "We Go High," Chance the Rapper provides some foundations for wisdom. The song begins with regret over foolish decisions and bad mistakes. As he says, "A new coat of paint don't make the stain go away."[10] He found himself unable to change. He needs something more or higher or deeper to deal with the stain of vice. He was beginning to see the warning of Proverbs: "There is a way that seems right to a man, but its end is the way to death" (Prov 14:12).

He gets the world's fame and honor in the second verse but still remains unsatisfied. "It's too bad, and it's so sad," Chance mourns in a bridge before the third verse. The resolution that he hints at between verse 2 ("We go higher") comes to fulfillment in the third verse. The search higher leads to the divine. With renewed energy and cadence, Chance the Rapper begins, "We give glory to you God. / One livin' true God makes us go Booyah." Death is the realization that something needs to change: "When time get rationed out, you get rational" (a continued warning, measure, and consequence throughout the book of Proverbs).

The broken relationship from the first verse is renewed in the last. The song ends with these lines: "We tried to form a new bar, just tell us what to do God." This end of love echoes the dependence needed in life. "Commit your work to the LORD, and your plans will be established" (Prov 16:3). The couple Chance pictures in the wedding vows redeems his pain. "By steadfast love and faithfulness iniquity is atoned for, and by the fear of the LORD one turns away from evil" (Prov 16:6). Marital love provides a sense of stability, satisfaction, and joy that does not culminate in itself but, as suggested, takes him higher to God—like a sacrament.

Killer Mike speaks of this same dissatisfaction in a life of vice and a greater satisfaction in a life of wisdom that Chance the Rapper showcases. "SHED TEARS" takes the Augustinian insight that "our souls are restless

---

10. Chance the Rapper, "We Go High."

until they rest in You"[11] and applies it to his own life. Over a gospel choir and piano, Lena Byrd-Miles sings, "I'm right here waiting to give you rest for your soul / When your soul needs peace, come unto me, I'll give you rest." Though culturally frowned upon for men to "shed tears," Killer Mike isn't afraid to confess. Throughout the song, he "sheds tears" for the troubles of life, the regrets, death, and the pain that accompany him. Yet, the promise of the chorus still rings, "Come unto me, I'll give you rest / Don't be afraid to rest."[12] Life is longing and unrest. Through wisdom and the wise, Killer Mike offers a different imaginary for happiness and wholeness through healing.

Waltke and de Silva propose that "in Proverbs, 'wisdom' mainly denotes the skill to navigate through the maze of life so that one conducts life to the greatest benefit of oneself and the community; it is the way of eternal life."[13] As such, there is also a communal shape of wisdom. "Put simply, the righteous disadvantage themselves to the advantage of the community; the wicked disadvantage the community to advantage themselves."[14] It's not merely about what is good for oneself but what is good for one's community. This wisdom emerges from a particular people and requires wisdom of elders.

This insight leads to another key feature of Proverbs, that of generational wisdom. Proverbs begins like a lecture to a son: "Hear, my son, your father's instruction, and forsake not your mother's teaching, for they are a graceful garland for your head and pendants for your neck" (Prov 1:8–9). The love of father to son results in the father wanting the best for his son. The relational bonds create a wisdom passed down.[15] In two different songs, Tobe Nwigwe enfolds a similar vision to that of Proverbs. Over a pared down, menacing track, Tobe ends the first verse of "FATHER FIGURE" with a refrain, "Not just a rapper to these rappers, I swear I'm they father figure."[16] Through proverbial wisdom, Tobe Nwigwe, along with Black Thought and Royce da 5'9", claims a superior status to the rap industry but for that of instruction rather than boasting. Such wisdom lies in lines like "Have some paper, but if you're known for hoin' your partners, you still big

---

11. Augustine, *Confessions*, 1.
12. Killer Mike, "SHED TEARS."
13. Waltke and de Silva, *Proverbs*, 28.
14. Waltke and de Silva, *Proverbs*, 236.
15. J. Cole's title for a track on his *2014 Forest Hills Drive* album is called "No Role Modelz," where he speaks about the dearth of good role models in his own life. For many, hip-hop artists become role models whether worthy of it or not.
16. Nwigwe, "FATHER FIGURE."

ol' trash" for those who boast in riches (Tobe in verse 1). Or "You lackin' humility, seekin' validity, shake the mistaken identity" (Black Thought in verse 2) for the prideful who claim "OG" (Original Gangster) status.

Likewise, in "MINI ME" Tobe joins Damian Lilliard (Dame D.O.L.L.A) and Tobe's wife (Fat) to offer more fatherly wisdom. The opening line from Tobe is "Peter Pan to these lost boys / They follow me." He goes on to speak of the trials of violence on the streets and peace within monogamy. Tobe's fathering a generation beyond his natural lineage, while Dame's verse is mainly directed to his own son. Regardless, they are concerned with those who follow them and emulate their actions. The chorus goes, "You are my mini-me."[17] They are claiming status as a sense of father to their community. Many celebrities—whether athletes or rappers—have this status whether they acknowledge it, desire it, or deserve it. The community looks up to them. Both urban and non-urban communities have a dearth of good male role models. Tobe Nwigwe is claiming the fathering status and desires to steward it well. Such sentiments are a key feature of Proverbs: passing on wisdom to a younger generation. Hip-hop needs father figures to shed light on the way. Virtue is taught mainly through modeling—having a "communion of saints" to emulate.

## HIP-HOP PROVERBS

> The way of a fool is right in his own eyes, but a wise man listens to advice.
> —Proverbs 12:15

Hip-hop has its own type of proverbs and wisdom. They speak into a particular location, drawing on generational wisdom to imagine a different future. It's a small, prophetic minority in mainstream hip-hop, but these artists speak powerful words. As Julius Bailey has noted, "Eschewing the superficial in favor of the substantive, the material in favor of the spiritual, the commercial in favor of the communal, conscious hip-hop is emancipating new generations of listeners and fostering communities of self-determined and self-aware individuals who are using hip-hop as a blade to cut through the empty promises of hyper-capitalism revealing the false promises that lurk at its core."[18]

17. Nwigwe, "MINI ME."
18. Bailey, *Philosophy and Hip Hop*, 61.

"DESTRUCTION" is one example where Tobe Nwigwe features Coast Contra as they speak wisdom while those headed for "destruction." Tobe raps about matrimony in the first verse and how some hear and desire it, yet they go to the club in search of a fling, "But everybody leavin' unfulfilled / When the thrill of the night is built on something fishy." In verse 2, Coast Contra warns about the danger of violence and anger, and they wish, "That'll one day listen to my wisdom for heaven sake / Was tryna guide you godly, you got in my way."[19] This wisdom can be heeded and lead to life, or it can be ignored and lead to "DESTRUCTION."

In "Gangsta Gangsta" by N.W.A., Ice Cube defiantly shouts, "Life ain't nothin' but bitches and money."[20] Old Testament scholar Richard Belcher argues that these are the two temptations of a young person that the book of Proverbs addresses: easy money and easy sex.[21] Hip-hop may often glorify these two temptations, but Tobe Nwigwe, Killer Mike, and Chance the Rapper offer alternative wisdom to the ways of the world. I'll draw on their work re-imagining money and sex and a few other proverbial topics they address in their music—namely, truth, violence, and examination.

## Proverb 1: Pursue Money but Don't Trust It

Long ago, W. E. B. Du Bois commented on the South's reconstruction and the model of Atlanta. He cautions this model where the dream of material prosperity is the touchstone of all success.[22] Further, he goes on to critique modern school systems where "instead of Truth, Beauty, and Goodness, wealth is the ideal of the Public School."[23] The desire for prosperity and easy wealth is not solely an urban phenomenon. In many ways, the American dream is a dream of upward mobility, material success, and comfort. The Bible, though, constantly warns against the temptation of prosperity.

Jesus says, "It is easier for a camel to go through the eye of a needle than for a rich person to enter the kingdom of God" (Mark 10:25). Paul cautions, "For the love of money is a root of all kinds of evils. It is through this craving that some have wandered away from the faith and pierced themselves with many pangs" (1 Tim 6:10). The author of Hebrews wrote,

---

19. Nwigwe, "DESTRUCTION."
20. N.W.A., "Gangsta Gangsta."
21. Belcher, *Finding Favour in the Sight of God*, 24.
22. Du Bois, *Souls of Black Folk*, 60.
23. Du Bois, *Souls of Black Folk*, 61.

## Part Two: Response

"Keep your life free from love of money, and be content with what you have" (Heb 13:5). These sentiments are found earlier in Proverbs, as well. When the fatherly figure addresses his son in Prov 1, the main direction is against a company of friends who would entice the son to ambush the innocent for material gain. The allure of money can be compelling. But here's the truth: "Such are the ways of everyone who is greedy for unjust gain; it takes away the life of its possessors" (Prov 1:19). According to proverbial wisdom, the good life may not be found in a prosperous life.

Easy money is often a temptation and feature of a "gangsta" life as N.W.A. described it earlier. Many hip-hop artists come from impoverished neighborhoods, so the allure of money and getting out of poverty is prevalent. In "BEEN BROKE," Tobe Nwigwe says that he's "been broke my whole life / Now money right."[24] With 2 Chainz and Chamillionaire, they discuss the benefits and freedom that money brings. Likewise, Chance the Rapper has a song called "Get a Bag." To an upbeat sample of James Taylor's "Only One," the chorus rings out, "You want a bag? You get a bag. / You need a bag? You get a bag."[25] With Calboy, Chance the Rapper speaks of similar desires, pursuits, and benefits that wealth brings.

The challenge is a desire for material stability without material dependency. The author of Proverbs asks the divine, "Two things I ask of you; deny them not to me before I die: Remove far from me falsehood and lying; give me neither poverty nor riches; feed me with the food that is needful for me, lest I be full and deny you and say, 'Who is the LORD?' or lest I be poor and steal and profane the name of my God" (Prov 30:7–9). Or, as Tobe Nwigwe indicates, the assignment is to "Get a lil' bag, get out the way, evade the hoes," while being aware "that paper in the air / Ain't gon' save your soul."[26] Wisdom is not opposed to wealth. Proverbs also says, "A rich man's wealth is his strong city; the poverty of the poor is their ruin" (Prov 10:15). It is a matter of trust, though, and stewarding the possessions one does acquire: "Whoever trusts in his riches will fall, but the righteous will flourish like a green leaf" (Prov 11:28). Wealth and "getting a bag" can be deceitful if that's the main purpose and goal to one's happiness. It's misleading without other ends. There are benefits to financial security, but perhaps, at times, hip-hop has oversold that promise.

---

24. Nwigwe, "BEEN BROKE."
25. Chance the Rapper, "Get a Bag."
26. Nwigwe, "GET A LIL BAG."

## Proverb 2: Monogamy Is a Blessing

In an article that analyzed rap lyrics regarding sex, a team of researchers found three major themes in *Billboard*'s top rap songs from 2001 to 2011. First, songs are about pursuing sex or nothing at all. In other words, sex is the only goal of the male–female relationship. If it's not leading to sex, there's no point in the encounter. The second common feature was the use of substances as a precursor or enhancer of the sexual encounter. Either alcohol or drugs are referenced as helping the experience along. The last theme they found was that sex was evaluated by the females' physical characteristics and non-verbal standards.[27] Females in hip-hop are often sexualized and only sexualized.

In 2020, Cardi B and Meghan Thee Stallion sent shockwaves through the radio waves with "WAP" (an acronym for which I can't bring myself to type out the meaning). Suffice it to say, it's as derogatory as many male hip-hop artists are about their sex life, but this time from the female perspective. Perhaps, Cardi B and Meghan Thee Stallion are claiming an equal independence from sexual mores, or perhaps we could hear it tongue in cheek: Do you hear what you sound like when you talk about sex this way? Regardless, in mainstream hip-hop, there seems to be dysfunctional wisdom regarding human sexuality.

Tobe Nwigwe and Chance the Rapper, again, prove models to picture a different vision of sex. Rather than sexual escapades, they present the beauties of married life. Tobe Nwigwe regularly raps with his wife, Fat, and has his children involved in music videos and shows. As he shouts in "FYE FYE," "If you book me for a show / And I can't bring my wife and my babies, I'm leavin.'"[28] He presents a vision of a faithful and present father who is not bothered by the ties that bind him to his family.

Proverbs consistently presents foolishness as the forbidden women. Virtue is presented as Lady Wisdom, as we will see, but the forbidden women tempt the young person. Proverbs 2 says the adulteress woman has smooth words and ways that lead to death (Prov 2:16–22). Imagining a spouse as living waters, Prov 5 encourages the young person to "drink water from your own cistern" for they are for you and not for strangers. The admonishment is to "rejoice in the wife of your youth" and be intoxicated with her love rather than the adulteress woman (Prov 5:15–20). Lady Folly

---

27. Johnson et al., "Thematic Analysis of Mainstream Rap Music."
28. Nwigwe, "FYE FYE."

is loud and seductive. She calls out and entices, yet these secret pleasures, Proverbs warns, lead to death (Prov 9:13–18).

Tobe Nwigwe explains his temptation with Lady Folly before his monogamous commitment. For Tobe, this vision is not some sentimental feeling. In "I CHOOSE YOU," he begins by saying that he doesn't believe in the concept of "in" love. The proverbial forbidden woman he names Whitni. When they kissed, he felt the flame of love. She was like the forbidden woman: loud and seductive but without life. Early in the song, Tobe raps that choices in the wrong direction have "the power to destroy your essence." But if love is a choice and not a mere feeling, then choices in the right direction can change him. As he goes on, "I got with Fat and low-key, she changed the trajectory of my vision / Supernatural circumcision from selfish ways, I'm on a mission."[29] Fat may not have had all the flame and sparks of "in love," but she had the depth that could change him. And as the song's title suggests, "I CHOOSE YOU" is about the choice of love which leads to life. *New York Times* columnist David Brooks defines maturity in a similar way: "It's the things you chain yourself to that set you free."[30]

Chance the Rapper takes a more romantic view of love in his recent album *The Big Day*, which is basically an ode to his wife and their new marriage. In "Found a Good One," the paired down beat and snare drum track repeats the female sung chorus, "I done messed around and found a good one. / Made just for me, yeah, made just for me," followed by Chance's repeated phrase, "I ain't single no more."[31] Proverbs has a similar statement: "He who finds a wife finds a good thing and obtains favor from the LORD" (Prov 18:22).

In "Eternal," Chance expounds on the superiority of faithfulness versus "side chicks." Jokingly, he raps, "Side chicks make they Kool-Aid with Splenda / Side chicks can't come to Auntie Linda's house."[32] He presents side chicks "Like a gold ring in a pig's snout is a beautiful woman without discretion" (Prov 11:22). Side chicks may look good, but they don't have the depth and substance of a faithful person. They can't even make Kool-Aid the right way. In a hip-hop world where sexual exploits and multiple partners are celebrated, Tobe and Chance imagine a different and better future. They present a better way of being in faithfulness and commitment to one spouse.

29. Nwigwe, "I CHOOSE YOU."
30. Brooks, "Be Really Good at Making Commitments."
31. Chance the Rapper, "Found a Good One."
32. Chance the Rapper, "Eternal."

Justin Bieber and Chance the Rapper released a single called "Holy"[33] in 2021. At first listen, I found my eyes glazing over with another "Jesus and me" love song put out by two well-meaning and sometimes profound popular artists. The refrain goes, "I feel so holy, holy, holy, holy / When you hold me, hold me, hold me, hold me, hold me." If nothing else, it seems they don't know what "holy" means. The reason Moses can't even look at God is because God is holy—much less be tenderly held by him. I've listened to my fair share of "How He Loves" and sloppy wet kisses. Even if it's not used in a worship service: hard pass.

But a second take, and especially with an eye to the music video, led me to consider something else happening. Sure, it's a popular song, and it nods to the romantic, generic love that will produce downloads. (Sex sells, after all). However, underneath, perhaps subversively, there's a message of desire, hopelessness, and the hospitable love of God—a love that awakens and welcomes.

In his book *Desiring the Kingdom*, James K. A. Smith argues that we are desiring creatures who are oriented to the good life by our ultimate love.[34] He says that advertisements—whether AXE body spray promising sexual desirability or a shampoo commercial pledging ecstasy at first use—understand this Augustinian secret: We are erotic creatures. If you want human beings to move, appeal to what they love. There's something about desire that pushes us along and pulls us outside of ourselves. Erotic love is not necessarily bad; to desire is human. The question is, "What is our desire pointed to?" *Agape* is rightly ordered *eros*.[35] Bieber and Chance offer a picture of rightly ordered *eros*—imperfectly but resolutely.

For instance, both performers' opening lines are indicative. Justin's first lines seem to be about more than romantic love: "I hear a lot about sinners / Don't think that I'll be a saint." Nevertheless, he plans to go to the river. Here, there's an obvious baptismal nod tinged with latent doubt. For whatever reason, he doesn't think he can be one of those "saints." When Chance's verse comes, he echoes the first lines of Bieber: "The first step pleases the Father / Might be the hardest to take." But coming out of the water, the tempo picks up: "I'm a believer / My heart is fleshy" echoing new birth and the replacement of a heart of stone with a heart of flesh (Ezek 36:26). There's something

---

33. I use the following from an article I wrote at *Mockingbird*. See Sosler, "Running to the Altar."

34. Smith, *Desiring the Kingdom*, 46–55.

35. Smith, *Desiring the Kingdom*, 79.

here about both their verses that are functioning allegorically: Yes, it can apply to marital love, but it's also about something more.

These lyrics point to the marriage supper of the lamb where marital love is a picture of the love of God. Chance returns to the fact that "I know when the son takes the first steps, the Father's proud / If you make it to the water, He'll part the clouds." As much as we'll stumble and fall, the Father looks and rejoices at the steps forward. He picks us up, dusts us off, and welcomes us back. And the promise: "I know I ain't leavin' you like I know He ain't leavin' us." There's something about this God that beckons him back. And then, "He holds me, holds me, holds me, holds me."

Considering this holy holding, against all better judgment, the bridge resounds: "They say we're too young and the pimps and players say don't go crushin' / Wise men say fools rush in."[36] Shouldn't we clean ourselves up first? Isn't this religion and God stuff all a bit rushed? Can't this be explained as an emotional fit? Don't you want to mature and grow a bit before you commit?

But when they come to the end of themselves and are desperate and lost, who will welcome them? "Holy" encourages us to run to the altar (a fitting word) like a track star. As such, they present marriage as a type of sacrament: their spouses are a way they encounter God.

## Proverb 3: Be True

Hip-hop is known for "keeping it real," or in modern terms, being "authentic." Artists express themselves and their experiences—good, bad, and ugly. I think this postmodern emphasis on authenticity distorts hip-hop's power. The modern quest tends to value expressing individual truth at the exclusion of the external good. The emotions have an elevated place, and the individual becomes the sole arbiter of truth. I want to extend that category of authenticity to more rightly name the "true" or "real." Hip-hop artists don't merely desire expression or authenticity. They value being true. Tobe Nwigwe has a song titled "BIG CAP" where he talks about being real in a culture of deception and lies. Rappers are chasing clout, but he sees the sham. "Some of y'all need a sombrero hat (why?) / Big, big, big, big, big, cap."[37]

Killer Mike speaks about the power of words and faithfulness in "HIGH & HOLY" (an albeit complicated title). He compares two generations: those that carry rifles and grannies that carry Bibles. He calls upon

36. Bieber, "Holy."
37. Nwigwe, "BIG CAP."

the ancient story of Cain and Abel to highlight an anger present in modern times. Rather than blaming it on his nature, he imagines another way of life: "high and holy." He's painting a picture of his life, making a difference even in the mistakes he's made. The way out of a life of destruction is confession. As he says toward the end of his last verse, "God bless those that confess and God damn the liars."[38] These lines feel harsh, but they're not too different from Proverbs: "Truthful lips endure forever, but a lying tongue is but for a moment. Deceit is in the heart of those who devise evil, but those who plan peace have joy. No ill befalls the righteous, but the wicked are filled with trouble" (Prov 12:19–21). We could read Killer Mike not pronouncing judgment but announcing the future reality. Rather than the culture of "cap" critiqued by Tobe Nwigwe, Killer Mike is "a hundred percent authentic, see I got no gimmicks / So I ain't protectin' no image."[39] He's not deceiving and wants to speak the truth, hard as it may be to hear.

## Proverb 4: Try Jesus, Don't Try Me

For the Christian, one of the more controversial songs from Tobe Nwigwe is "TRY JESUS." In a gospel-sounding track, the refrain is "Try Jesus, don't try me"—that is, if you mess around with me or mine, "I throw hands." One part of the singing track bellows, "Oh, He said, 'Turn the other cheek' / Oh, but that's one part of the Bible, that don't just sit right with me."[40] One could read this as a justification for violence and a rejection of Jesus' teaching.

However, the song could also be read as a type of self-examination and confession. That is, "I know myself, and this is my warning to you." Hip-hop music is not absent of violence or guns. In Killer Mike's "SCIENTISTS & ENGINEERS," he announces, "I am a menace that's movin' on vengeance / I promise my opp that my anger is endless."[41] James Baldwin once wrote, "I imagine that one of the reasons people cling to their hates so stubbornly is because they sense, once hate is gone, that they will be forced to deal with pain."[42] This anger and pain in the hip-hop community may lead to a more tense community. As Grandmaster Flash said in "The Message,"

---

38. Killer Mike, "HIGH & HOLY."
39. Killer Mike, "SCIENTISTS & ENGINEERS."
40. Nwigwe, "TRY JESUS."
41. Killer Mike, "SCIENTISTS & ENGINEERS."
42. Baldwin, *Notes of a Native Son*, 103.

"Don't push me cause I'm close to the edge."[43] As such, Tobe's invitation to "Try Jesus" may just be an invitation knowing his own limitations.

There's also a protective element to Nwigwe's warning. He's not going to start anything. He's not glorifying violence. He is promising protection for himself and his family. He won't hit first, but he may hit back. So, "Try Jesus."

## Proverb 5: Self-Examination

At the heart of all three artists is an honest self-examination. Modern culture distracts us and deceives us. We're too busy to take an honest look. We have too many external pursuits and are trying to "get a bag." One of the powerful elements of prophetic hip-hop artists seems to be the ability to take stock of their culture and themselves to live in the present more faithfully. As mentioned in the introduction, they are world-makers more than advice-givers.

In Killer Mike's recent album *MICHAEL*, his elder reflections come in full force. Reeling from the death of his mom and grandma, he's offering up a wise perspective of an elder brother. Already noted in "SHED TEARS," I discussed his openness to mourn the losses of his life, while still hoping and choosing toward a brighter future. He doesn't shift the blame to his environment but notes its powerful pull. He takes responsibility for his life. "It was me, I'm the reason that I fell." Pride is the reason he assigned for his rise, but it led to his fall. It was only in his humility, his shedding tears, that he "made it to the mountaintop straight from the valley of sin."[44]

This humility is also shown in "SOMETHING FOR JUNKIES." Rather than standing over junkies in a self-congratulating stance, he learns, "When you see men fall, don't laugh / Learn, learn because you're on your way up."[45] To laugh is "to make the same mistake yourself"—to pretend like you're immune from temptation. Killer Mike has learned the lesson of Proverbs: "When pride comes, then comes disgrace, but with the humble is wisdom" (Prov 11:2). Those who are suffering, the junkies, are fellow human beings and, therefore, should be shown mercy and grace rather than judgment and condemnation. Killer Mike needed to walk through some things and examine his life to gain a perspective from humility. He invites us to withhold judgment with him.

43. Grandmaster Flash and the Furious Five, "Message."
44. Killer Mike, "SHED TEARS."
45. Killer Mike, "SOMETHING FOR JUNKIES."

## CONCLUSION

In "5 Year Plan," Chance the Rapper takes stock of his life. He's reviewing his life and sees the beauty of his given life. He realizes that the blessings of his life have sometimes been through missteps. "The heart of man plans his way, but the LORD establishes his steps" (Prov 16:9). He advises, "There's no time for impatience in your five year plan / You got time for hesitation in your five year plan." Sometimes, our best plans need interrupted. So, "if you followed your flight plan, you'd be right here prayin.'"[46] He then confesses the Lord of lords who gives abundantly. It's a call to plan, but there's also a givenness to the blessing of life that goes beyond our planning. Even the best Proverbs fall back on grace.

Time and space fail to include others like Lupe Fiasco, Nas, Tupac, or J. Cole. This chapter is a small spattering and a few proverbs we could glean from listening to hip-hop. In some ways, they align with traditional Proverbs. In other ways, they challenge or add layers to our understanding. In all of them, they follow the tradition of black artists who present a different imagination to the world, a prophetic future, a call to wisdom.

## BIBLIOGRAPHY

Augustine. *Confessions*. Translated by R. S. Pine-Coffin. New York: Penguin, 1961.
Bailey, Julius. *Philosophy and Hip Hop*. New York: Palgrave Macmillan, 2015.
Baldwin, James. *Notes of a Native Son*. Boston: Beacon, 2012.
Belcher, Richard. *Finding Favour in the Sight of God: A Theology of the Wisdom Literature*. Downers Grove, IL: IVP Academic, 2018.
Bieber, Justin. "Holy." Featuring Chance the Rapper. Track 5 on *Justice*. Def Jam Recordings, 2021.
Bilbro, Jeffrey. "The Taste of Strawberries: Tolkien's Imagination of the Good." *Christ & Pop Culture Magazine: Beauty's Allure*, Aug. 8, 2014.
Brooks, David. "Be Really Good at Making Commitments." *Time Magazine*, June 16, 2015. https://time.com/3922993/david-brooks-graduation-speech-dartmouth/.
Chance the Rapper. "5 Year Plan." Featuring Randy Newman. Track 15 on *The Big Day*. Self-produced, 2019.
———. "Found a Good One (Single No More)." Featuring SWV and Pretty Vee. Track 19 on *The Big Day*. Self-produced, 2019.
———. "Get a Bag." Featuring Calboy. Track 16 on *The Big Day*. Self-produced, 2019.
———. "We Go High." Track 5 on *The Big Day*. Self-produced, 2019.
Du Bois, W. E. B. "Criteria for Negro Art." http://www.webdubois.org/dbCriteriaNArt.html.
———. *The Souls of Black Folk*. Mineola, NY: Dover, 2016.

46. Chance the Rapper, "5 Year Plan."

## Part Two: Response

Fiasco, Lupe. "Rap Theory and Practice: An Introduction." YouTube video, Dec. 6, 2022. https://www.youtube.com/watch?v=zBHRsYhYb-0.

Grandmaster Flash and the Furious Five. "The Message." Track 7 on *The Message*. Sugar Hill, 1982.

Greenidge, Kaitlyn. "Black Spirituals as Poetry and Resistance." *New York Times*, Mar. 5, 2021. https://www.nytimes.com/2021/03/05/t-magazine/black-spirituals-poetry-resistance.html.

Hodge, Daniel White. *The Soul of Hip Hop: Rims, Timbs and a Cultural Theology*. Downers Grove, IL: InterVarsity, 2010.

Johnson, Kimberly, et al. "Thematic Analysis of Mainstream Rap Music—Considerations for Culturally Responsive Sexual Consent Education in High School." *Journal of Applied Research on Children: Informing Policy for Children at Risk* 8 (2017) article 8.

Killer Mike. "HIGH & HOLY." Featuring Ty Dolla $ign. Track 14 on *MICHAEL*. 2023.

———. "SCIENTISTS & ENGINEERS." Featuring Future and Eryn Allen Kane. Track 7 on *MICHAEL*. VLNS LLC/Loma Vista Recordings, 2023.

———. "SHED TEARS." Featuring Mozzy and Lena Byrd-Miles. Track 2 on *MICHAEL*. 2023.

———. "SOMETHING FOR JUNKIES." Featuring Fabo. Track 11 on *MICHAEL*. 2023.

McWhorter, John. "How Hip-Hop Holds Black Back." *City Journal* (Summer 2023). https://www.city-journal.org/article/how-hip-hop-holds-blacks-back.

N.W.A. "Gangsta Gangsta." Track 3 on *Straight Outta Compton*. Ruthless Records, 1988.

Nwigwe, Tobe. "BEEN BROKE." Featuring Chamillionaire, 2 Chainz, and Fat Nwigwe. Track 6 on *moMINTS*. Self-produced, 2022.

———. "BIG CAP." Featuring Fat Nwigwe. Track 9 on *moMINTS*. Self-produced, 2022.

———. "DESTRUCTION." Featuring Coast Contra. Track 3 on *moMINTS*. Self-produced, 2022.

———. "FATHER FIGURE." Featuring Royce da 5'9" and Black Thought. Track 4 on *CINCORIGINALS*. Self-produced, 2020.

———. "FYE FYE." Featuring Fat Nwigwe. Single, *FYE FYE*. Self-produced, 2021.

———. "GET A LIL BAG." Featuring Fat Nwigwe. Track 5 on *moMINTS*. Self-produced, 2022.

———. "I CHOOSE YOU." Track 7 on *THE ORIGINALS*. Self-produced, 2018.

———. "MINI ME." Featuring Dame D.O.L.L.A. and Fat Nwigwe. Track 10 on *moMINTS*. Self-produced, 2022.

———. "TRY JESUS." Featuring Jabari Johnson. Single, *TRY JESUS*. Self-produced, 2020.

Otteson, K. K. "RZA on the Current State of Hip Hop: 'The Wisdom Is Missing.'" *Washington Post*, Apr. 5, 2022. https://www.washingtonpost.com/magazine/2022/04/05/rza-wu-tang-clan-hip-hop/.

Smith, James K. A. *Desiring the Kingdom: Worship, Worldview, and Cultural Formation*. Grand Rapids: Baker Academic, 2013.

Sosler, Alex. "Running to the Altar with Justin Bieber." *Mockingbird*, Oct. 14, 2020. https://mbird.com/music/running-to-the-altar-with-justin-bieber/.

Van Leeuwen, Raymond. "Wisdom Literature." In *Dictionary for Theological Interpretation of the Bible*, edited by Kevin Vanhoozer et al., 826–29. Grand Rapids: Baker Academic, 2024.

Waltke, Bruce, and Ivan de Silva. *Proverbs: A Shorter Commentary*. Grand Rapids: Eerdmans, 2021.

# Part Three

## Testimony

# 7

# Why?

## A Theological Reflection of Jadakiss's Most Thought-Provoking Questions

### Nicole Hudnell

If it weren't for The Bronx, this Hip-Hop thing would never be going on, so I'm going to tell you where I'm from... Uptown Baby, Uptown Baby, Uptown Baby!

—Lord Tariq and Peter Gunz, "Déjà Vu"

Two individuals from the Bronx wrote and recorded these words from "Déjà Vu": Lord Tariq and Peter Gunz. I could not help but reference them, because, like me, they highlight an area where I was raised. In hip-hop, it is customary that we celebrate where we are from. Traditionally, hip-hoppers rep (represent) their 'hoods (neighborhood) or the block they lived on as they were coming of age. It is only fitting to honor that tradition by telling you a little about myself.

I am a Black woman from the Bronx, New York. I was born and raised in the uptown sections of Wakefield and Williamsbridge. Like most kids in the Bronx, I grew up in a single-parent home. My mother raised my sister and me all by herself. My mother grew up in Far Rockaway, New York, Interestingly—it is a long way from the Bronx. I would joke and question, "How did she end up over here?" When I finally mustered up the courage to ask, the answer made sense.

My mother and her four siblings grew up in Far Rockaway, a small Queens, New York, area. When my mother was thirteen, they moved to Columbia Heights in Harlem, New York. After her mother passed away, they all moved out and went their own way. The oldest, my Auntie Pam, moved back to Far Rockaway; Uncle Tim was married and moved to Columbus, Ohio; Uncle Steve was in Brooklyn; and sadly, my Aunt Josephine passed away shortly after my grandmother. My mother moved to the Bronx. Going to the Bronx was dangerous when my mother was growing up. She told me stories about how my grandmother would forbid them to go to that borough in New York City. At the time, the Bronx was nothing but crime, poverty, gang activity, and drug infestation. My grandmother did not want her children anywhere near the Bronx, but due to unfortunate circumstances, that's where my mom ended up, and I am glad she did.

At the age of thirty, my mother had my older sister, Shayla. My mother, my sister, and our father lived in a one-bedroom apartment until two years later when I came. Needing more space, they moved to a two-bedroom apartment on 238th and Nereid Ave. My father was long gone when I turned three, and my mother did everything independently. I do not have any memories of him; I would not be able to tell stories about who he was or what he did. Honestly, I did not know I did not have a father. Most of my friends did not either, so I didn't feel fatherless. As I continue this chapter, I will explain how being a daddyless daughter impacted my hip-hop theology.

My mother would wake up early every Saturday morning and clean our home. I remember my sister and I would wake up to the scent of Pine Sol filling the air and soul music, setting the tone for a typical weekend for the Hudnell Family. My mother was washing the dishes in the kitchen, and I went there to talk to her. As she was washing the dishes, she was singing along to the music on the radio when she suddenly dropped the plate, rinsed her hands with water, and ran into the room to turn up the volume. I followed her because I did not understand why she wanted to hear this song playing louder than the last few on the radio. She began to rap along with the lyrics. At the time, I did not know rap because my mother did not play anything like that. She played gospel, jazz, R&B, and soul music.

## Why?—Hudnell

I grew up hearing Luther Vandross, Anita Baker, Whitney Houston, and Barry White. I was curious to know who this new voice was and what he was doing with his words.

"Mom, what is this? Who is this?" I spoke.

"Pete Rock and CL Smooth, they are a rap group," she replied.

Waiting for clarity, I looked at her, hoping she would say more, and she did.

"It's called T.R.O.Y., They Reminisce Over You. CL Smooth is the rapper, and Pete Rock made the beat," she elaborated.

"What does that mean?" I inquired.

"The song is about his life; to reminisce is to think back, so the song is him rapping about his childhood."

I was intrigued.

I was intrigued for many reasons. First, I did not know my mother could rap (or try to rap). The second reason was that I learned a new word. *Reminisce* was a new word to me, and I loved the definition. I loved the idea that when one is reminiscing, they are taking the time to reflect on their lives and all they have been through that made them who they are. Lastly, I understood what it meant to tell one's story. I liked that I understood who CL Smooth was just by listening to his lyrical storytelling. I enjoyed hearing about the memories he shared and how the people in his life played an essential role in his upbringing. From the lyrics, I quickly realized we had so much in common. At nine years old when I first heard the record that day with my mother, I recognized similarities, and I noticed some later in my adulthood. That day began as an ordinary Saturday morning and changed my life forever simply because I asked a question. I wanted more. I wanted more of whatever that was. I wanted to feel that again: listening to a song, resonating with the words, and finding myself. I did not know it then, but hip-hop became the father I never had.

The male voices I heard rapping those lyrics told stories and shared truths about what it means to grow up in the struggle—navigating survival, joy, love, hurt, and pain—while also raising thought-provoking questions about education and religious perspectives. Hip-hop has a way that encourages listeners to challenge their thinking. The questions invite the listener to think about issues that must be addressed because they have been ignored long enough. Hip-hop, as a predominantly African American and Latino music genre, mimics the interests of its people. Whatever we care about, hip-hop cares about. Hip-hop concerns itself with issues that matter

## Part Three: Testimony

in African American and Latino culture. In hip-hop, you'll hear about the Black and brown experience; you'll be able to close your eyes and imagine, even for a second, what it means to grow up Black or brown in America. It reflects the stories of our people, both past and present, and how they shape and impact our future. Some stories, we understand. Some are de facto; whether correct or not, it is what it is. Some need a little bit of explanation. We know the who, the what, the when, the where, and maybe even the how. It is the *why* that always gets us; the real question is, are you ready for the answer?

The feeling I got when I learned the word *reminisce* was the start of my love for words. I like words. I want to know the definition of words and where they come from. I did not realize it, but I became interested in etymology from an early age. When I heard an unfamiliar word, I would grab the nearest dictionary and look up that word. I remember when I would ask my older brother how to spell something, he would always say, "Sound it out." When I got older, I would ask my mother for the definition of a word, and she would always give me an example rather than a concrete definition. At the time, I didn't like her way of responding to my inquiry because it was too basic. I wanted a scholarly response that I could repeat in class, and the teachers would think I was the most brilliant student they'd ever met.

It was important to me to sound like an intelligent young person, and there is one reason for that. My mother spoke very well. My mother always told my sister and me about her mother and how refined and elegant she was. My grandmother Essie Bailey worked at Columbia University. After leaving Queens, my mother and her siblings moved into a predominantly white neighborhood not too far from Columbia University, and it was important to her that her five children spoke well, communicated effectively, and didn't say "ain't."

As I began writing this chapter, I recalled a conversation with my Auntie Pam about my grandmother. To ensure I remembered correctly, I asked my aunt, "Why didn't my grandmother like the word 'ain't'?" My aunt reminded me that my grandmother was an educated Southern woman. She loved books and learning about culture; her children needed to speak proper English. I made it my mission to speak well, have a strong vocabulary, and understand the etymology of words in honor of my grandmother.

In his book on etymology, Yakov Malkiel defines the term this way: "Etymology always meant something approximately to the paraphrase, 'original meaning, or use, of a given lexical unit or proper name.'"[1] Most words, if not all, have an origin refined and established over time. Let us consider the adverb *why*. Research shows that Old English *hwi* indicates for what purpose or by what means.[2] While the spelling of the adverb has changed over time, the original meaning has been maintained. When people ask *why*, they are doing so to gain some clarity or understanding of what they are asking about. As human beings, it is natural to inquire about the unknown. We need answers; we want answers.

Like most young people, I had a lot of questions. I wanted to know something about everything. There was a time when I got in trouble because of questions. I did not get in trouble because I asked the questions but because I did not settle for the answer I received. I recently came across a book called *3 Big Questions That Shape Your Future: A 60 Day Exploration of Who You Were Made to Be*.[3] The book was written for a young audience. It assures young people that they are not alone in their quest to understand the world around them. It encourages them to ask questions. Kara Powell writes, "Questions take us on a journey, and the act of exploring, wondering, seeking, even wrestling our way towards answers change us."[4] We are naturally curious people; we want to know how and why the world functions the way it does and what it all means for us in the end—the pursuit of finding the answers to those questions drives us. Asking and being asked the right question can inspire a person to consider self-evaluation in an area of their lives that calls for radical change. As believers, sometimes we ask each other questions that will position us for optimal success in our faith formation, but what about when we dare to question God?

God welcomes questions. Too often, when people give their lives to Christ, they are instructed not to question God. They are told they are to walk by faith and not by sight, meaning that even if they have questions about where they stand as Christians, they are left with unanswered concerns. John Hopper writes, "I'm sorry to say, however, that Christians often can be of little help when it comes to the 'whys' of Christianity. Not only can they find themselves short on good answers to good questions, but sometimes they also make it clear they aren't comfortable with you even

---

1. Malkiel, *Etymology*, 1.
2. Etymonline, "Why."
3. Powell et al., *3 Big Questions That Shape Your Future*.
4. Powell et al., *3 Big Questions That Shape Your Future*.

asking your questions in the first place."[5] The idea that it is not okay to ask questions always puzzles me especially when (some) believers conveniently leave out all the individuals in the Bible who asked questions. Let us focus on two of the most powerful questions in the Bible—one in the Old Testament by Habakkuk and the other in the New Testament by Jesus.

Habakkuk was a prophet. During his time, the Babylonians were victorious at Carchemish and would proceed to consolidate their control over Syria-Palestine.[6] Habakkuk's prophecy resulted from these events. He believed in God and showed his faith whenever he went to pray before the Lord. He knew all about God and his wondrous works (Hab 1:1–3). Everything you just read is straight outta seminary. I want you to understand all that I am about to say. I told you I am from the Bronx, so this is my opportunity to speak to you the way I would if I was talking to the homies, but I'm going to make it into a Bible study.

If you read Habakkuk, you will agree that he was brave. He did not hesitate to ask God the tough questions surrounding sin and injustice. When he didn't understand all that was happening around him, he didn't keep quiet; he talked with God. His questions were direct and unfiltered, with no sugarcoating or effort to soften their impact. Frustrated, he asks, "Why do you make me look at injustice? Why do you tolerate wrongdoing? Destruction and violence are before me; there is strife, and conflict abounds" (Hab 1:3 NIV, here and throughout). To put it in layman's terms, Habakkuk was saying, "God, you know I am a prophet, and I have these visions. I see so many things that are happening that should not happen; why do you allow me to see it in my prophecy?" He was also asking, "Why aren't you stepping in where so much is happening?" There was so much turmoil, calamity, destruction, and everything you can think of, but God allowed it to continue for some reason. Habakkuk was a sensitive guy. He knew that God does not like sin. It pained him to see all that was happening, and he couldn't understand why God would allow him to get the prophecy when he couldn't do anything about it and when he felt like God wasn't doing anything about it. The why question we have been discussing in this chapter is evidence of the etymology of the adverb. When we ask why, it is to question the purpose of. When Habakkuk asked God why he saw the injustice, he wanted to know God's purpose for giving him those visions.[7]

---

5. Hopper, *Questioning God*.
6. Collins, *Introduction to the Hebrew*.
7. Barnes et al., *Ultimate Commentary on Habakkuk*.

His question was raised out of confusion and perplexity. Anyone who asks questions is asking to get a response. Habakkuk was no different; he asked, and God answered. Although God decided to respond to Habakkuk in the Old Testament, he remained silent when Jesus questioned him in the New Testament, the second powerful question I want to consider.

The heart of Christianity is the belief that God took on human flesh by sending his only begotten Son into the world (John 3:16). Jesus came to earth to save sinners because sin was the source of every pain felt by humans. While Jesus was on the cross dying for our sins, he cried out to God, questioning, "My God, My God, why have you abandoned me?" God was silent. So many people read this verse and want to know why God ignored the cries of his Son while he was in the most pain. I want to focus on the question rather than the absence of the answer.

Across the four Gospels, Jesus asked a total of 307 questions. Some of the questions were about longing; some were about compassion; some were about identity; some were about faith; and others were about doubt. Isn't it interesting, however, that the last words Jesus spoke before he died were in the form of a question, and that was about distress? Martin B. Copenhaver writes, "And yet, the question Jesus asks on the cross is different from all His other questions. It is not a rhetorical question or a teaching tool. It is not offered for the benefit of Jesus' hearers. Rather, it is an agonizing question that is difficult to hear. This question is raw and threatening, like an open wound. It sounds like an expression of despair, of hopelessness, of doubt even, which, of course, is just what it is. And it hangs in the air unanswered."[8]

On the cross, Jesus took on the sins of the world, and for the first and only time in his life, he was separated from God. He asked the question, but he did not get an answer. Sometimes in life, we ask God the why questions. Why am I still struggling? Why am I not married yet? Why should I continue to pray, and I have yet to hear a response? When Jesus was on the cross, crying out to God, asking what I think is the most significant why question in the Bible, God remained silent. Some may even say God abandoned him. The hardest part to accept, however, is that the only thing that separated Jesus from God was when he took on sin that wasn't even his. The beautiful part of it all is that he did so because he loves us, and by taking on our sin, we would never have to be separated from the Father.

---

8. Copenhaver, *Jesus Is the Question*.

## Part Three: Testimony

Habakkuk questioned God and received an answer. Jesus questioned as well but did not receive a reply. Sometimes, our questions are answered, while others are abandoned. Religion tells us that we are not to question God, while theology highlights the moments in the Bible when some of the most influential figures did and how their inquiries influence our faith formation. I think questions are essential to living a complete life. Questions indicate that we are interested in what is happening around us. Like Habakkuk, we have questions about injustices; like Jesus, we ask questions while in affliction. I know I am not the only one who has had Habakkuk and Jesus moments when questioning God. We have all, at some point, asked God why. Whether it was trying to get clarity or wanting God to step in because of our suffering, we ask questions.

Let us consider hip-hop. Hip-hop artists are some of the most curious individuals on the earth. They are creative enough to develop rhymes on a beat while their minds are racing and filling up with questions about the world they need answers to. In 2004, Jason "Jadakiss" Phillips, one of hip-hop's elite rappers, released a song asking all the why questions concerning the state of Black America.

Full disclosure: Jadakiss is one of my favorite rappers. In my opinion, if you are a hip-hop connoisseur, Jadakiss has to be considered one of the Top 5 Dead or Alive. Throughout his career, he has managed to move listeners with his four-line build-up, powerful punches, witty bars, storytelling capabilities, and thought-provoking questions. His song "Why" was one of the most impactful records released in hip-hop culture. It dropped during a time when Black Americans were experiencing controversy concerning politics, mainstream media, social injustices, and even religious biases. In the original and the remix, Jadakiss asks some of the most thought-provoking questions concerning injustices, social inequalities, God, and love.

The music video for the song begins with a voice-over from a news anchor on the television. There are short clips that quickly cut from what looks like a protest scene, war footage, a telecommercial, a glimpse of police brutality against a Black man, and more. As he flips through the channels and shortly after cutting off the television, Jadakiss, sitting comfortably on a chair, looks directly into the camera and shouts, "Let's get real!"[9] The beat drops, and the questions begin. The visuals lead us in to the questions that Jadakiss will "get real" about: social injustices, inequalities, and all things plaguing Black America.

9. Jadakiss, "Why."

## WHY IS THE INDUSTRY DESIGNED TO KEEP THE ARTIST IN DEBT?

The business part of hip-hop has always been questionable. Artists have expressed frustration with the lack of legal representation when negotiating business deals and branding themselves to make enough money to feed their families. The Black and brown artists have been lowballed and tricked into thinking they are making good money when, in fact, the music industry and labels behind them have been the financial beneficiaries of their creativity and intellectual property. While discussing the lack of fairness or justice in the music industry, Drew Schwartz from *VICE* writes, "While some deal structures are inherently more equitable than others, there's no getting around the fact that the odds are stacked against most artists from the get-go. Artists find themselves deep in the red before they even arrive in the studio to record . . . but it doesn't have to be that way."[10] Jadakiss is an artist, so it was bold of him to question the industry or those in power who possibly have some control over his career. It makes me wonder how fed up a person would have to be to question the machine behind them publicly. He is not guessing or speculating about the relationship between the industry and the artist. The industry was designed to keep the artist in debt, and he wants answers.

## WHY NIGGAS CAN'T GET NO JOBS?

I apologize in advance if that word triggers you. I could have used asterisks for the four letters in the middle, but I wanted to preserve the authenticity with which I believe Jadakiss asked the question. It is no secret that Black people in America have experienced unequal treatment in the workplace for years. The labor experience for Black Americans has been significantly worse than that of their white counterparts. Unemployment is extraordinarily high in the Black community.[11] The disparity between whites and blacks, as it pertains to job obtainment in America, is indicative of the oppression from which we need liberation. James Cone's Black liberation theology advocates for racial justice from the experience of the oppressed, the oppressed being Black people.[12] By asking the question, Jadakiss sheds

---

10. Schwartz, "Bad Deals Are Baked Into."
11. Pitts, "Bad Jobs."
12. Cone, *Black Theology of Liberation*.

light on the systemic exclusion and discrimination of Black people in the labor market. It seems like a fly-by question, but it is deeply rooted in the desperate need to question why Black Americans, whose ancestors built this country, still struggle to earn substantially gainful employment.

Jadakiss was brave enough to ask these controversial questions to the powers that be. He recognized the injustices artists were experiencing and decided to incorporate the question in the lyrics. His inquiry about why Black people don't get jobs was fully loaded. I think even the fact that he decided to use the term *niggas* was liberatory. Society says we are not supposed to use that word, but whoever said that must not understand Black history at all. It is in our nature to take everything that was supposed to be used against us, reclaim it, re-own it, and use it for good. Like Habakkuk, when Jadakiss couldn't tolerate the immorality around him, he addressed it. He asked the most controversial questions that concern Black America in the most personal ways. Both Habakkuk and Jadakiss asked their questions with deep concern about the possibility that justice was being ignored.

Initially, I only wanted to focus on the original record, but I realized the remix has a few more theologically embedded questions. Rappers Styles P, Common, and Nas are guest features on the remix.

Styles P questioned, "Why we still gotta pray to Allah?"

Common asks, "Why I gotta have religion if I believe in God?"

Nas inquires, "Why is Jesus Christ never played by Black actors?"[13]

These are all worthwhile questions to consider—especially in a volume on theology and hip-hop, but I want to keep pondering the questions from Jadakiss.

## WHY IS IT THE MONEY MOTIVATES ME, BUT THE LOVE KEEPS ME GROUNDED?

People enjoy discussing love in the capacity of friendships, relationships, intimacy, and God. In addition to the question in this "Why" remix verse, Jadakiss has a compelling relationship with love. When he mentions love, he often indicates that he believes love must be balanced with something else. On one record, he says, "I told him the money will never equal to the love,"[14] or "Soon as the money gets right, that's when the love change,"[15] or

---

13. Jadakiss et al., "Why (Remix)."
14. Jadakiss, "Still Feel Me."
15. Jadakiss, "Child Abuse."

lastly, "The real gonna win, the fake gonna lose, love overpowers the hate by twos."[16] It appears that love cannot stand alone. While love can be balanced with money, love cannot be overpowered by hate.

In the Black community, there is often this crab-in-a-barrel mentality. It is the idea that "If I cannot do it, neither can you" or "You cannot have more than me; you cannot succeed ahead of me." Hip-hop emcees tell their stories or refer to personal and impactful situations in their lives. It appears that Jadakiss may have suffered quite a few losses in his friendships or relationships when he became financially sound. Consequently, he concludes that it is not uncommon that the love one receives may be predicated upon how much money they have. He realizes that in some cases, there will come a point when one may have to choose between the two. Jadakiss, however, chooses love.

On the "Why" remix, Jadakiss asks a very thought-provoking question that gets overlooked compared to the others, but theologically, it is worth expounding upon. He asks, "Why is it the money motivates me but the love keeps me grounded?"[17] There is so much to unpack.

"C'mon, let's be truthful; who doesn't enjoy having a couple of extra dollars in their back pocket? Black people often experience higher levels of economic insecurity than any other subculture in America."[18] Within the Black community, being financially anchored is something to aspire to; everyone wants to get to a point in life where they no longer have to worry about money or where their next meal will come from. One can only assume that Jadakiss has seen some financial freedom, even if artists do not always get what they deserve from record labels. At the very least, we can assume that he makes more than others in his home community.

How is it that money motivates him, but love keeps him grounded? When exegeting the book of Mark, we must remember that while Jesus conversed with the disciples, he predicted his death. He told listeners that if anyone wants to be his follower, they must take up their cross and follow him. He goes on to say that one should not hold on to the life they have but instead be willing to lose it for the sake of being one of his disciples. The most satisfying Scripture, when connecting to the question asked by Jadakiss, reads, "To what does it profit a man if he gains the whole world but loses his soul, is anything worth more than your soul?" (Mark 8:34–37).

16. Jadakiss, "Who's Real."
17. Jadakiss, "Why."
18. Pitts, "Bad Jobs."

Jesus condemns those who desire to gain the world or worldly things such as money at the expense of their soul. Some people will give up true, genuine love if it means being rich or wealthy. This faulty mindset is frowned upon because Jesus teaches that, above all else, we must be willing to love just as he has loved us (John 13:34–35). There is more to life than money, riches, and wealth. Apart from the hit song "Money, Power & Respect" by The LOX where each artist emphasizes the importance of respect (instead of love) over money, I think Jadakiss recognizes that truth.[19] When he raps about money and love being unequal, money altering the love one receives, but how love overpowers hate, he implicitly says that love conquers hate and defeats money. When he notices that money may motivate him (because we need to be financially responsible), it is not strong enough to overpower love or keep him from being grounded. The love keeps him focused, honorable, respectable, teachable, and even desiring to ask questions to seek knowledge and understanding.

These probing questions are one of the reasons that I am a huge Jadakiss fan. I truly respect his thought process and his desire to seek understanding. I enjoy listening to his music and seeing the Godhead in his lyrics. I find myself thoroughly dissecting his lyrics and making the correlation between what he is saying and the Scripture I believe serves as an undergird for his thought process. Aside from the lyrics in the song "Why," Jadakiss is often met with questions about the complexities of the Black experience and what it means to come into a relationship with the Lord. On another record he has with fellow hip-hop emcee Nas, who was on the remix, they continue their series of questions, but this time by asking *what if?* That would be another fruitful exploration of theology and hip-hop.[20]

## CONCLUSION

Earlier in the chapter, I wrote about my Uncle Tim. I forgot to mention that he is also a bishop. As a bishop, he mentors, teaches, and counsels those in need. In a sermon, he described this powerful encounter he had with one of his congregants, which I believe illustrates how asking and being asked the right question can change a person's life trajectory.

A woman came into his office in distress. She told him about her hardships and all she was experiencing at the time. Feeling downhearted, with

---

19. The LOX (ft. DMX and Lil' Kim), "Money, Power & Respect."
20. Jadakiss (ft. Nas), "What If."

tears filling her eyes, she weeps, "The devil is throwing everything at me but the kitchen sink!"

He questions, "Why are you here?"

Reiterating what she had already poured, she said again, "The devil is throwing everything at me but the kitchen sink!"

In his last attempt to get the response he sought, Bishop Timothy J. Clarke repeats, "Why are you here?"

At this moment, Bishop Clarke was operating in a leadership role. He asked this question as a leader to ignite a response that would later bring about change. In his book detailing the lessons he's learned as a leader in the workplace, Dr. Steve Adubato offers a practical guide for individuals to learn how to be influential leaders. In the chapter "Great Leaders Ask Great Questions," he writes, "How leaders go about confronting is key to what happens next and, ultimately, how difficult situations are resolved—or not. These questions—the worried and the judging ones—put people in a position to either fight back or clam up."[21]

At this time, the question was about more than geographical location. Bishop Clarke wasn't asking why she was there as in what prompted her to seek his counsel. He was not asking her why she was there to say she didn't need his advice or words of encouragement. He was, however, asking why she was there in a physical and emotional state. He wanted her to reflect, assessing her physical location and how her presence in his office stopped her from getting what she needed. She needed the devil to throw everything at her AND the kitchen sink. Once the kitchen sink was thrown, the enemy had nothing left, and she would be free to begin taking her life in a new direction.

As believers, we are not promised a life of bliss. Nothing in the Bible says life will be smooth once we accept Jesus Christ as our Lord and Savior. We are going to have struggles and feelings of despair. Sometimes, it may feel like all life offers is sadness and sorrow with no hope for a liberating tomorrow. I would, however, offer the Scripture Ps 30:5, which reads, "Weeping may endure for a night, but joy comes in the morning." Weeping symbolizes the temporary suffering one may feel while undergoing trials and tribulations. What the lady Bishop Clarke counseled was going through at home was weeping; once she got through the night, or metaphorically speaking, having the kitchen sink thrown at her, she should expect to welcome joy.

---

21. Adubato, *Lessons in Leadership*.

## Part Three: Testimony

I can almost guarantee she felt helpless when she entered the office. After that one seemingly simple question, she probably left feeling ready to take on whatever came her way because she knew that her time to smile again was coming soon.

I love hip-hop. I am in love with hip-hop. I am in love with the elements, the art of storytelling, and how an emcee can relay a message in the most creative ways possible, but most of all, how God shows up in hip-hop. When I fell in love with this genre of music, I had no idea I would use it as a teaching tool for myself and even for those around me. Earlier in the chapter, I mentioned that I did not have a father. Hip-hop filled that space. The male voices I heard served as the role model which my young ears desperately needed to hear. Their words of wisdom and thought-provoking questions prompted me to ask my own. When I got saved at the age of twenty-one, I had many questions about God, and because I didn't have a father who raised me in the church, the only theological discourse I had was with hip-hop. Growing up in the 'hood, we have theological conversations without even knowing; it's authentic. All it takes is for one person to randomly shout out, "Yo, y'all know Jesus ain't white right?" and there goes the conversation. Black people will sit for hours and converse about what is true and what needs some explaining; however, it all stems from their desire to gain some understanding of who God is and what he has done for the marginalized and underserved communities. We involuntarily become hip-hop 'hood theologians. Ralph C. Watkins explains, "The Hip-Hop 'hood theologian is the re-embodiment of Dr. James Cone in the present-day context. They are young, as he was, back in 1968. The Hip-Hop 'hood theologian is a prophet who speaks truth to the powers within the African American community and outside it. The willingness to have multiple theological conversational partners has given the Hip-Hop 'hood theologian a broader audience that appreciates their moving beyond religious tolerance to theological inclusion."[22] That's what hip-hop does. Hip-hop challenges listeners to shift their thinking and go against the status quo. Hip-hop is encouraging because it leads one into a space of problem-solving, critical thinking, and analytical reasoning in the context of hip-hop and theology. Hip-hop wants to know that there is a God that looks like them. Hip-hop wants to know that God will appear in the secular space without fear of losing sacredness. Hip-hop wants to know that there is a God that shows up for the underrepresented. That God is willing to go in and advocate for the

---

22. Watkins, "From Black Theology and Black Power," 337.

profane despite being spiritually profound. As a hip-hop theologian, I hope to continue to do the work that will make Dr. James Cone proud. Hip-hop theology is deep; it represents those of us in the 'hood who love God and hip-hop, and that's something that needs no questioning.

## BIBLIOGRAPHY

Adubato, Steve. *Lessons in Leadership*. New Brunswick, NJ: Rutgers University Press, 2016.

Barnes, Albert, et al. *The Ultimate Commentary on Habakkuk: A Collective Wisdom on the Bible*. N.p.: e-Book, 2016.

Collins, John J. *Introduction to the Hebrew Bible and Deutero-Canonical Books*. Minneapolis: Fortress, 2014.

Cone, James H. *A Black Theology of Liberation*. Maryknoll, NY: Orbis, 2020.

Copenhaver, Martin B. *Jesus Is the Question: The 307 Questions Jesus Asked and the 3 He Answered*. Nashville: Abingdon, 2014.

Etymonline. "Why." https://www.etymonline.com/search?q=why&utm_campaign=sd&utm_medium=serp&utm_source=ds_search.

Hopper, John. *Questioning God: Answers to Questions Worth Asking*. Fort Worth, TX: Search Ministries, 2021.

Jadakiss. "Child Abuse." Track 2 on *The Champ Is Here, Pt. 2: Kiss My Ass*. Def Jam Recordings, 2008.

———. "Still Feel Me." Track 12 on *Kiss of Death*. Interscope Records, 2004.

———. "What If." Featuring Nas. Track 8 on *The Last Kiss*. Ruff Ryders, 2009. https://genius.com/Jadakiss-what-if-lyrics.

———. "Who's Real." Track 3 on *The Last Kiss*. Ruff Ryders, 2009.

———. "Why." Track 6 on *Kiss of Death*. Interscope Records, 2004.

Jadakiss et al. "Why (Remix)." On *Kiss of Death*. Ruff Ryders/Interscope, 2004.

The LOX. "Money, Power & Respect." Featuring DMX and Lil' Kim. 1998. https://genius.com/the-lox-money-power-and-respect-lyrics.

Malkiel, Yakov. *Etymology*. Cambridge: Cambridge University Press, 1999.

Pitts, Steven. "Bad Jobs: The Overlooked Crisis in the Black Community." *New Labor Forum* 16 (Dec. 2007) 39–47. https://doi.org/10.1080/1095760601113373.

Powell, Kara Eckmann, et al. *3 Big Questions That Shape Your Future: A 60-Day Exploration of Who You Were Made to Be*. Grand Rapids: Baker, 2022.

Schwartz, Drew. "Bad Deals Are Baked Into the Way the Music Industry Operates." *VICE*, Oct. 21, 2020.

Watkins, Ralph. "From Black Theology and Black Power to Afrocentric Theology and Hip Hop Power: An Extension and Socio-Re-Theological Conceptualization of Cone's Theology in Conversation with the Hip Hop Generation." *Black Theology* 8 (June 9, 2010) 327–40. https://doi.org/10.1558/blth.v8i3.327.

Williams, Justin. "Historicizing the Breakbeat: Hip-Hop's Origins and Authenticity." *Song and Popular Culture*, 2011, 133–67.

# 8

# The Theology of Suffering and Songs for This Age

### Stephanie Laferriere Greer

"The sting of death on this side of eternity is more like an anvil weighing down on a tattered feather held only by strands of grace. For the days where it feels like death has won, I'm pleading for my savior's comfort."[1] I wrote that phrase over and over again in my journal a couple days after my brother John had passed. The reality that God is in control, even in the midst of suffering, is a great comfort, but pain still hurts. On March 4, JFury, or John as he was known by me, was hit by a large vehicle as he crossed the street. I got the call early the next morning, and as I sat in shock, nearly five months pregnant, I started to realize the loss. He wouldn't get to meet my son. We would never exchange another YouTube video with a good song. He never got to meet my husband. My parents would have to bury another son. I cried out to the Lord and could only read the Psalms. I knew that they spoke of great loss, and they also forecasted great redemption. The truth of Ps 56:3–4 reigned true: "When I am afraid, I put my trust in you. In God, whose word I praise, in God I trust; I shall not be afraid. What can flesh do to me?" (ESV throughout). When my mind could not entertain any more

---

1. Greer, "When Death Hits Home."

questions, I went to the simple memories to fill the gaps. He loved walking, and he loved walking at night to clear his head. I'm not sure what he was thinking about that night, but I'd like to think that he was freestyling as he crossed that country road. I'd like to think that he came up with a hook and would be running home to pen it on paper and send me a photo of his journal filled with pencil marks that had been erased. In those days to follow, I'd play hip-hop songs that he loved just to feel like he was still here, and it brought comfort.

Our last song exchanged was Octave Minds featuring Chance the Rapper's song "Tap Dance." We loved this song with its elements of dance, the fast lyrics, the musical arrangement, and the themes present. "Tap Dance" brought up a couple themes: living in this world but being aware that there is one to come, and the overall lesson of pressing forward to the next step. Over and over again the chorus repeats "one, two, one, two" to show the quickness of the next movement of life and of dance. "One foot in the door, one foot in the grave . . . One-two, one-two, one-two, one-two, step one-two, one-two, step."[2] I would fake tap dance and he would rap along; we felt close as we didn't agree on everything but didn't need to in order to connect. Hip-hop helped.

Twista's fast raps always had us on a roller coaster trying to match the music with the lyrics. John and I would do the vocals to Twista's "Hope"[3] and dissect Twista's words of lament during suffering. Twista's perspective in that song is him looking toward a better world, and it gives him encouragement to live in the present. John and I related over these desires for our world. We wanted to see a hopeful impact in our neighborhoods and in our words.

I can't speak about hip-hop without speaking about John. Due to struggles with addiction, we had a complicated relationship toward the end of his life. He began to get clean and return to the things he once loved before addiction numbed him. We were mending our relationship on the basis that God does, in fact, give second chances. I'm not exactly sure why God would choose to take him in this way, especially considering all the ways he had spared him prior. I do know that the mercy of God had reached JFury's life, and, in the midst of the wreckage, God is still good. "We are safe. God, in his holiness, is keeping us and showing mercy to us.

---

2. Octave Minds ft. Chance the Rapper, "Tap Dance."
3. Twista, "Hope."

## Part Three: Testimony

We may not be aware of it, but it is true. He is with us even in the deepest and darkest pit."[4]

They called him JFury. I called him John. His real name was John Peter and he would claim me as his kid sister most days. Growing up, every couple of days, he'd call me downstairs to show me a new move he mastered. Or at least he thought he mastered it. I remember he'd grab his Kangol hat, his AIWA boombox, and his mat and attempt to do another headspin. I was the hype man, making sure to be louder in my encouragement than in my laughs. "What strange creatures brothers are."[5] After enough headspin attempts and the clock reminding us that we forgot to pull out the meat from the freezer AGAIN, we'd scramble to figure out how to have the microwave work its magic undetected. Spoiler alert: We never figured it out. With fifteen minutes to go until Mom pulled up, we scrambled, tossed the toys into the playroom, stopped playing *Mortal Kombat* on the Sega Genesis, and pushed our dirty laundry into the crevices we could find under the bed. We divvied up tasks: I started washing dishes, while John began vacuuming in spaces we shouldn't have been that day, especially that living room where no one was to enter except for once a year. We left the star symbol on the floor, complete with an aroma from the deodorizer, but not too much or else Mom would know we turned the house into Jumanji while she was gone. There was one common denominator in all of the chaos, and it was the beats in the background. Our days were curated by hip-hop music. It was one of the only constants of our days.

I can't speak about hip-hop without speaking about JFury. My introduction to hip-hop was primarily through him. He often picked what we listened to, and I was along for the ride, just happy to be in his presence. We grow more in love with something when someone we deem important values it. We also grow more in love with something when it gets taken away. The journey of suffering is for everyone who has breath, though in different degrees, it is the language everyone knows.

When Nas released "Ether" in 2001, we were going through all the bars and waiting to see what other diss tracks would be next. The Roots, A Tribe Called Quest, Biggie, and Eminem were on heavy rotation. His favorite was DMX, hailed as the only artist to make number 1 on the *Billboard* charts. DMX, born Earl Simmons, had a rawness as he discussed addiction, the struggle with temptation, pain, and his hopeful expectation of a better

---

4. Piper and Taylor, *Suffering and the Sovereignty of God*, 185.
5. Austen, *Pride and Prejudice*, 42.

life. He had some club hits for sure, but the ones we were always drawn to were the lyrics with heart behind the beat.

There's beauty in knowing that there is truly nothing new under the sun; God in his wisdom would provide a book of poetry, hymns, and prayers that ask the deepest questions and leave his people with true hope. These God-breathed inspired words that God gave to its writers are a compilation of poetry, pleas for provision, petitions, and proclamation of God's goodness during times of deep sorrow and great rejoicing (2 Tim 2:16–17). Spanning over the course of one thousand years, the Psalms were compiled by the Israelites from the time of Moses and would be gathered for generations after.[6]

Music has long since been a balm for sufferers. In every genre, we find a divide between the mainstream hits and the music that we listen to when we're contemplative and by ourselves. Hip-hop sings the song of the sufferer and speaks of hope, conflict, vengeance, and redemption. The opportunity to communicate emotions, regrets, and hope for resolve is found in the bars laid out over various beats. It's therapy without trips to an office; it's closure without having to have a conversation. The theology of suffering finds its home first in the pages of the Bible from Hagar to Joseph, from Mary to John. The Bible isn't foreign to the ills of the people. There are songs of suffering for this age, and hip-hop presents the struggle of making it through the everyday moments of life, from celebrations to discouragements.

## HOW I MET HER

I couldn't tell you the etymology of hip-hop or how it originated, but I know what it meant for immigrant children in Brooklyn—back when being Haitian wasn't cool, when we wore Sunday's best to every occasion; whether it was a normal day at school or we were heading to church, my parents were adamant that we would give our guests our best. Athleisure only had its place in the home after church and when we were all heading to bed. Growing up Haitian meant extracurriculars were reserved for church meetings and youth groups. It was back when you had to sneak any kind of music that wasn't classical or Kirk Franklin. My pores smelled like castor oil, and my lunches filled the air wherever I ate with maiz moulin (corn) and poisson (fish). Before people in the mainstream cared about Toussaint Louverture or the beastliness of Haiti becoming the first black republic, it was hard to be Haitian in America. Being black didn't give me any sense of

---

6. Plumer, *Psalms*, 8.

Part Three: Testimony

belonging in our predominantly African American community. We still felt like outsiders; hip-hop gave us a place where we could all relate. It was our common ground. Though different in ethnicity, culture, and nationality, hip-hop listeners found themselves among friends when we were drawn to the substance and wordplay. Though different, we knew the song of suffering and hip-hop would meet us at the crossroads of why.

## QUESTIONS

Our family had been accustomed to death; it was an unfortunate friend. John and I first encountered death together when our brother Vladimir collapsed and stopped breathing on a summer day in 1993. Vladimir was my older brother and John's younger brother; when he died we grieved in different ways, but collectively we were devastated. The specifics were blurry for me as a four year old, but one thing was clear: we would be left forever changed on that day.

We encountered suffering and would come to the question, why? Some answers would come later, but the full understanding of the why wouldn't come. We knew that much. Amid extreme heartbreak, we were drawn to looking for meaning in spite of our sufferings. This search for meaning was not reserved for my brother and me; it is the cadence of the whole world. Hip-hop helped us through the feelings that accompanied the loss of our brother, but there was still something missing. What truths would anchor us as we processed guilt and shame from that day?

"See, to live is to suffer. But to survive. Well, that's to find meaning in the suffering."[7] The opening lines of DMX's "Slippin'" presents the question that many other hip-hop artists pose in their songs. It is first a declaration that every human being suffers and then a plea for meaning. The plea for meaning is only found during enduring various forms of suffering. Whether big or small, tragic or inconvenient, suffering has us ask ourselves two questions. What makes our suffering meaningful? Why do we still attempt to survive? If you haven't suffered, you haven't lived. DMX understood the dilemma: he had a desire for living, yet he saw the conflict that suffering would bring, and still he had longings of peace that he would come to fight for in the middle of all his sufferings.

One thing is true: We are always at a crossroads with suffering. No one living is immune. Our world, though beautiful, has been impacted by

7. DMX, "Slippin'."

the reality of missing God's mark. We are impacted by the consequences of distorting God's image and his image bearers. Sin's introduction ruined everything and caused true unrest and peace. We did not choose righteousness on our own, and we can't be made right with God on our own merit (Rom 3:23). Though we did not know Adam and Eve, we come from them and are also awaiting the return of our Savior whose arrival will bring us peace again. Peace with God and peace among men.

## TWO FUNDAMENTAL QUESTIONS

## Why Suffer?

> Lord Jesus, you have brought me from a place so dark
> To the point where I can now feel the love in my heart.[8]

DMX, like so many of us, searched for this hope and experienced true hope on this side of eternity. Hope is present in his lyrics as he reflects on being in deep darkness and the difference when he encounters God's love for him. Throughout the various lyrics listeners can see DMX's freedom and security to ask the hard questions. "Slippin'" presents the question of why people suffer. His understanding of this broken world agrees with God's word in saying globally we suffer because of the presence of sin. Our world is impacted by sin, and we sin collectively. We have no hope until we place our hope in the crucified Savior who shed his blood on the cross for sinners who call out to him for forgiveness. Hope is the reason people endure suffering. They believe that it is better to pursue life than to die. The desire is innate; it's God-given. Earl, the man behind his stage name DMX, presented this desire to strive toward hope in his song. The lines in his first stanza state that he's looking on for better days. He pursued trivial desires, and it resulted in fractured relationships with his kids, with friends, with the development of his craft, and in struggles with past addictions. His grit and honesty are evident through each line; his content is explicit, but he made known his need for Christ. He was honest with his listeners about his need for Christ.

John and I had a complicated relationship. We were five years apart, and I spent most time trying to be just like him, but also unlike him, so I couldn't be compared. In my eyes he often did things bigger and better. Growing up, we fought about everything else besides hip-hop. We wouldn't

---

8. DMX, "Prayer."

grow closer until I realized I could lose him. Suffering helps you appreciate that which is worthy to be held close. He signed up to serve in the Marine Corps in 2002. He was deployed to Iraq shortly after basic training. I did not know the reality of war, but the possibility took me back to loss.

## IT WAS GOD

In the beginning, God saw everything that he had made, and he declared that it was very good (Gen 1:31). There can be no talk of suffering before dwelling on the goodness of the world before sin entered it. Things were good, really good—perfect. God and man dwelled together in harmony. God created us to reflect his image, to steward the world he created (Gen 1:27–28). The minute sin entered the world was the beginning of suffering. "Underlying all trauma, violence and abuse lies evil, and the result of evil is always some kind of suffering."[9] The separation caused by disobedience and falling into the serpent's trap would be the event that would be forever referenced by mankind. Sin separates us from God; it separates us from anything good because God is the truest form of good there is. Every human being must come to terms with the consequences of our sin, both individually and corporately. In order to truly find hope, every human being must be reconciled to the creator who offers hope through his Son, Jesus. The entrance of evil ruined everything, and the world is tainted by sin. Hagar hides her son, so that she does not have to see him die of starvation; Joseph is sold into slavery, is betrayed and forgotten; Mary sees her son crucified on the cross for the sins of the world though he is innocent; John, who is credited to be the disciple whom Jesus loved, is exiled to a foreign land and waits for the return of his Messiah. Evil doesn't just happen on a singular level. Suffering addresses communities and people.

## Does God See?

> Knowin' even when we're suffering, He sees us
> Or when you're lost, He will lead the flock to find the one[10]

---

9. Langberg, *Suffering and the Heart of God*, 29.
10. DMX, "Prayer."

## The Theology of Suffering and Songs for This Age—GREER

DMX alludes to the story of Jesus being the good shepherd, one who knows all of his kids and seeks to sacrifice his life to ransom them from ultimate damnation (Luke 15:4–5). He, in turn, argues that God is good; he is worthy to be trusted. It would be insanity to put one's hope in a god who does not rule all and is incapable of acting. It would be even more insane to submit to a god who calls us to follow up and endure suffering but has no plan of hope for his people. We live in the tension of knowing that God is in control and everything happens by his permission, and he commits to working it out for our good. The character of God isn't diminished in our struggles to understand the complexities between God's omnipotence and human suffering. As pastors John Piper and Justin Taylor state, "He is never absent or inactive when human beings hurt each other or themselves. In the person of his Son, he is always in our midst, as the one who holds each and every aspect of creation, including all of its evil aspects, in his hands so that he may carry it to where it accomplishes exactly what he wants."[11] The God of Abraham, Isaac, and Jacob is omniscient and omnipotent, meaning that he can see all things and he is the only all-powerful one (Gen 50:24).[12] The Psalms speak the same truth; "Great is our Lord, and abundant in power; his understanding is beyond measure" (Ps 147:5). The Psalms assert that God does all he pleases, that he is in control (Ps 115:3). God knows each of our thoughts; he knows us better than anyone and isn't unaware of what troubles us.

Grief changes you. As I look back on John's life I thought about how the trauma that he had endured would subtly show itself in the form of apathy or dissociation. Holidays were the worst as he tried to grasp the reality that life had been given to him where it was taken from others. Fireworks celebrated America's holidays, and all John felt was rage and guilt. God saw John through in the years to come; he would be able to celebrate his daughter's smile or the joy of a simple walk down the street without ducking. Though he was changed, he began to see that his struggles only made him more useful in speaking into the lives of at-risk youth. He poured his life out altruistically to help others. Sometimes, it was his joy; other times, he would be seeking penance. The way we'd relate to each other would change. We were not the same, but hip-hop met us at a crossroads. "Yo play this track, it's so good, just the wordplay of it hits." John would often leave me voicemails, if I didn't answer, with the song in the background. In our adult

---

11. Piper and Taylor, *Suffering and the Sovereignty of God*, 65.
12. See Frame, *Doctrine of the Word of God*, 66.

years we had differences in our preferences on how to live in romantic relationships, smoking preferences, and friends. I had become a Christian and had begun to ask questions that the Psalms began to answer. It became a new type of song for me, and I'd hoped to share it with him in hopes that he, too, would behold and put his hope in Christ too.

> And when I came back you accepted me with open arms and said "All is forgiven."[13]
> I come to you hungry and tired, you give me food and let me sleep[14]

DMX's transparency before God is counterculture in the hip-hop world. Where most brag about their wealth and power, DMX was raw and honest in his need for strength. He admits his humanity, and he presents his weaknesses. His calling God the good shepherd means he knows that when you come to God, there is truly nothing we lack. John told me of a time when he was lying down in his barracks and heard the voice of our brother Vladimir. It was loud and clear: "Get up, right now!" As their base was bombed, not all of his friends were spared. He suffered from a great deal of survivor guilt as a result of so many close calls with death. "God must want me alive, he keeps saving me even when I'm hoping to die," he confessed. His despair was great; the realities of war are horrid.

It's common to doubt being loved, especially when we wrestle with the past. God saves those with checkered pasts, with memories so horrible it haunts them. There's no amount of hell that humans can go through that's deeper than God's ability to find them and offer healing. Not only does God save salvifically through his Son, but he also offers present-day saving, moment-by-moment saving. After the war, we spoke a great deal; we wrestled with the depths of love and forgiveness Christ offered to those who would confess. While JFury related to the rhymes signifying our fallen condition, he was more drawn to the God to whom DMX prayed. DMX had been so open about his downfalls; he was so bold about his need for forgiveness. For John he was able to see that strong men could also be afraid, needy, and humble about something as personal as salvation. Through DMX's struggles with drugs, feelings of worthlessness, past traumas, and failures, John saw himself. If God could save a man like DMX, he could save a man like John. He related to him in a way that he didn't relate to anyone else in

---

13. DMX, "Prayer."
14. DMX, "Prayer."

his life. John had resolved that "the miseries of the unconverted are inconceivably dreadful. Over them depravity reigns; guilt loads their souls with its fiery chains."[15] He would come and submit to the one who provides a hiding place for him in the middle of the storm.

## A NEW SONG

Death reminds us of the curse of sin, but it also reminds us to look toward the day when God will make it right again. "He will wipe away every tear from their eyes, and death shall be no more, neither shall there be mourning, nor crying, nor pain anymore, for the former things have passed away" (Rev 21:4). God has used hip-hop, particularly the rhymes and life of DMX, past failures, past traumas, freedom, to ask the hard questions to display two facts. One, that we must come to terms with our sin, and two, we can only find true solace from our Savior, Jesus Christ. God sees, forgives, and saves. That reality was true not only for DMX, or my brother, but Christ extends it to all who come (Rom 10:9). Christians believe that our Savior is the Living One—that he died on the cross and resurrected three days later (1 Cor 15:3–4). He has completed the will of the Father for the glory of God (John 6:38). The question of whether God sees is answered in countless Scriptures where we rejoice that God has seen the plight of the sufferer. He is aware of all that ails them, and he watches over their lives (Ps 146:6–10). Those who endure walking with the Lord can rejoice at the revelation that Christ will come back and make all right again. They were singing a new song before the throne (Rev 14:3). Matthew Henry so beautifully states, "Christ is with his church and in the midst of her in all her troubles, and therefore she is not consumed. It is his presence that secures her perseverance."[16] I'm not sure what beat will accompany this new song, though I can imagine harps—and drums! It'll be the song we sing and replay over and over again, far surpassing *Billboard* records, better than any cipher I've ever heard. Its bars will be sung by the redeemed. Those who have tasted and seen God's forgiveness and love lavished onto them! The tunes produced by the voice of the people whom God has kept bring me great joy, and I live longing for that cadence, for that chorus we will all sing. Till then, we endure knowing the truths about God in the songs he provides in this age even in hip-hop.

---

15. Plumer, *Psalms*, 405.
16. Henry, *Matthew Henry's Commentary on the Whole Bible*, 2479.

## Part Three: Testimony

Themes presented in hip-hop songs of substance cause us to examine questions that people have in regard to suffering and pain. The Christian worldview would confidently assert that while we are unable to answer all of the nuances that suffering brings, its inception occurred when our ancestors, Adam and Eve, committed the first sin. In that moment in the Garden of Eden, we find the first glimmer of hope and compassion; God speaks, and man still lives (Gen 3:6, 9). We see that Adam calls his wife Eve, which means mother of all the living, God's provision (Gen 3:20). The ultimate mic-drop moment occurs when God promises that the snake crusher will bruise the head of the serpent (Gen 3:15). Christ is the snake crusher, and this isn't just relegated to imagery in an ancient book; it is the reason why we can have hope in our suffering! It's the reason we can weep, repent, and restart. It is because of the person of Christ, his condescending to earth, living a perfect life, submitting to the Father, dying on the cross for our sins, and inviting us to renounce our past ways and place our trust in him. Secular hip-hop presents great questions, but it comes short of a solution for dealing with the troubles of life. The search for the wellspring of continual hope is only found in the one who knows all the answers.

## BIBLIOGRAPHY

Austen, Jane. *Pride and Prejudice*. 1813. Repr., New York: Penguin Classics, 2003.

DMX. "Slippin." The Island Def Jam Music, 1998. https://www.youtube.com/watch?v=9Ww-TQUeA3E.

———. "Prayer (Skit)." The Island Def Jam Music, 2012. https://genius.com/Dmx-prayer-lyrics.

Frame, John M. *The Doctrine of the Word of God*. Phillipsburg, NJ: P&R, 2010.

Greer, Stephanie Laferriere. "When Death Hits Home." *The Adventures of a Mahogany Girl* (blog), Mar. 23, 2021. https://mahoganyadventures.wordpress.com/2021/03/23/when-death-hits-home/.

Henry, Matthew. *Matthew Henry's Commentary on the Whole Bible*. Peabody, MA: Hendrickson, 2017.

Langberg, Diane. *Suffering and the Heart of God: How Trauma Destroys and Christ Restores*. Cork: LSC-NewGrowthPress, 2015.

Octave Minds ft. Chance the Rapper. "Tap Dance." YouTube video, 2014. https://www.youtube.com/watch?v=v8VUXTivlr4.

Piper, John, and Justin Taylor. *Suffering and the Sovereignty of God*. Wheaton, IL: Crossway, 2006.

Plumer, William S. *Psalms: A Critical and Expository Commentary with Doctrinal and Practical Remarks*. Carlisle, PA: Banner of Truth Trust, 1975.

Twista. "Hope." Track 7 on *Coach Carter: Music From the Motion Picture*. Atlantic Recording Corporation, 2004.

www.ingramcontent.com/pod-product-compliance
Lightning Source LLC
Chambersburg PA
CBHW031458160426
43195CB00010BB/1017